SPARK

EDITED BY

ELIZABETH WONG

JOANNA WONG

ALDEN E. HABACON

SPARK

THE INSPIRING LIFE
AND LEGACY OF
MILTON K. WONG

GREYSTONE BOOKS

Vancouver / Berkeley

*Dedicated to the next generation of inspired
leaders and all those committed to the compassionate
stewardship of our planet and its people*

Greystone Books Ltd.
www.greystonebooks.com

Cataloguing data available from Library and Archives Canada
ISBN 978-1-77100-440-4

Editing by Barbara Pulling
Copy editing by Shirarose Wilensky
Design by Peter Cocking and Jessica Sullivan
Jacket photograph by John Sinal Photography Inc.
Photography of Wong art collection by Dave Robertson Photography Inc.
Family photographs courtesy of the Wong family
Printed and bound in China by 1010 Printing Group Ltd.
Distributed in the U.S. by Publishers Group West

Every effort has been made to trace ownership of visual and written material used
in this book. Errors or omissions will be corrected in subsequent printings, provided
notification is sent to the publisher.

We gratefully acknowledge the financial support of the Canada Council for the Arts,
the British Columbia Arts Council, the Province of British Columbia through the
Book Publishing Tax Credit and the Government of Canada through the Canada
Book Fund for our publishing activities.

Greystone Books is committed to reducing the consumption of old-growth forests
in the books it publishes. This book is one step towards that goal.

Frontispiece: The brothers in front of Modernize Tailors.
(From left to right) Maurice, Jack, Milton, Bill and Allan.

Contents

Foreword

WHEN I WAS asked to write the foreword for this tribute to Milton Wong, it seemed like a project. It was Milt himself who asked me; he knew the book was underway during the last year of his life. By that time, he and I had known each other for fifteen years and developed a friendship from what started as a solicitor/client relationship. The full weight of my obligation, though, hit home as I stared at the blank page and considered the task—to communicate in a few words the essence of a book that chronicles the legacy, forged over more than seven decades, of an extraordinary person. The ironic twist in all of this, which probably explains, in retrospect, Milt's mischievous grin, is that he knew he was the person I would usually consult on something like this. And this time around, he would be unavailable.

The book you are about to read is a collection of vignettes fashioned to reveal the intrinsic Milton Wong. Get ready to be impressed. Milt was a delightful individual and someone who figured largely in the lives of many, many people. The *New York Times* published an interview last year with an accomplished venture capitalist who laid out five questions a mentor should ask his or her mentee: What is it that you really want to be and do? What are you doing well that is helping you get there? What are you not doing well that is preventing you from getting there? What will you do differently tomorrow to meet those challenges? How can I help? Milt understood the significance of these questions instinctively, and he applied them hither and yon, whether you liked it or not. In fact, you could become his mentee without really knowing it until it was too late.

It is a nifty gift to be able to see clearly the strengths and weaknesses in another person. Whether Milt approached you or you approached him, he reached into your psyche and aligned your values with his to make you stronger, faster, better. He believed those values should be mined in everyone to advance the human condition.

All facets of society were game for Milt's boundless energy, but I believe his true passion was social justice. He was not satisfied with what he viewed as intermittent dollops of mercy. Instead, he relentlessly pursued deep and positive structural changes to the "system."

Milt had a long-time friend who postulated that humans are motivated by goodness, glory and gold—the three Gs. Milt and I spoke of this one morning in 2008 as we floated on a guillet in a small bay with turquoise waters off the coast of Turkey. I had coaxed him to get up and experience the Mediterranean at dawn, its ethereal beauty and the optimism that inspires. We marvelled at the grand sweep of history this place had seen. The Egyptians, the Greeks, the Macedonians, the Romans, the Mongolians and the Crusaders, among others, had all at one time or another had a go at it.

The circumstances were particularly evocative for us as amateur philosophers. As the sky's lemon and lime hues changed to magenta, periwinkle and then azure, we discussed these marauders and empire builders and what had driven their actions. Eventually I asked Milt to consider, using rough percentages, to what extent each of the three Gs underpinned his own actions in life. He declined to answer, offering me a wry smile instead. Here's my conjecture, though, based on my many years of knowing Milt. Gold was definitely important to him, but only as a means to an end. He couldn't wait to give away, for example, in a burst of philanthropic exuberance, the small fortune he'd made on the sale of his shares in ALI Technologies. He did like glory, but mostly for the inspirational effect it had on others. So goodness was dominant. In fact, if Milt had a flaw, it was that he hadn't processed adequately Bob Dylan's admonition on his *Infidels* album that "sometimes

Satan come as a man of peace." Although he always saw the goodness in people, during his last year Milt shared with me how perplexed he was by the actions of some people he had misjudged.

On that Mediterranean morning, our conversation meandered, but somehow Milt found his way into my dome, as he always did, with a gentle inquiry: "So, what are you going to do with the rest of your life? You need a legacy." I was feeling very peaceful at the time, so I didn't get too rattled, but part of me felt like a snowshoe hare with a bobcat on its tail. Many of those who knew Milt will recognize that feeling, and we wouldn't have it any other way.

Enjoy this book. SPARK doesn't just celebrate a great person; it prompts introspection, a quality Milt prized. I expect you'll find that reading this chronicle of Milton Wong's life will make you stronger, faster, better…

GEORGE BURKE
JULY 17, 2013

George Burke is a lawyer who has practised for thirty-three years. He is a husband, father and grandfather, and beyond those accomplishments, as requested, he is shaping a modest legacy.

Milton and his father,
Wong Kung Lai.

Milton K. Wong
A Life in Brief

M ILTON K. WONG was a visionary who made the impossible seem possible. He had a relentless passion and a deeply rooted sense of social values that helped to shape Canada into a more diverse, innovative and just nation. When Milton passed away from pancreatic cancer on New Year's Eve 2011, he left behind a vibrant legacy of contributions in the public and private sector, the arts and the social justice community.

Born in Vancouver, British Columbia, on February 12, 1939, Milton was raised in the closely knit community of Chinatown alongside his eight siblings. His parents had emigrated from China in the early twentieth century. His father, Wong Kung Lai, became a tailor and eventually opened his own shop, which he called Modernize Tailors. From an early age, commitment to community was an integral part of Milton's life. He watched his father's involvement in local Chinese organizations and accompanied his mother, Man Ming, on her visits to help the disadvantaged in their church community. For many years, Kung Lai also brought over countless "relatives" from China. These people remained part of the Wong family until they had established their own roots in Canada.

Even as a boy, Milton had a huge amount of energy and drive, getting up at 4:00 AM to go around town helping the milkman. Like his brothers and sisters, he spent part of every summer at Camp Artaban, an Anglican camp on Gambier Island, and it was there he developed his lifelong appreciation of nature. Transportation from Vancouver was via Union Steamship, and campers and luggage were deposited on a floating dock in the middle of

the bay. From there, they were rowed to the campsite. Milton loved athletics such as rugby, and his high-school track and field club, the Optimist Striders, became one of the most powerful youth athletic clubs in Canada. Even as a busy adult, Milton was fond of plunging spontaneously into physical challenges such as triathlons and half-marathons.

Family was always important to Milton. He began dating his future wife, Fei, when they were both living in Toronto. In 1968, they married and began their incredible journey together. Milton was actively involved in the lives of his three daughters, Andrea, Sarah and Elizabeth; his sons-in-law, Kevin Joe and Joseph Meyler; and his three grandchildren, Matthew, Tyler and Katherine.

Milton had a gift for bringing people together, and he took great joy in sharing the outdoors, food and laughter with loved ones. He taught his children and grandchildren to fish, play tennis, bike, cook, bake and, most importantly, have fun. Although Milton's work took him around the world, he was happiest when he returned to Taku, his family resort on Quadra Island. He cherished his walks there along Rebecca Spit with Fei and their dog, Rudy. Milton was proud to see his dream home at Taku, complete with a green roof, become a reality.

▲◄ Milton with his daughters, Sarah, Elizabeth and Andrea, getting ready for Halloween.

▲ Rudy the dog, Milton and Fei enjoying their favourite place on Quadra Island.

◄ Milton planning his living roof.

▲ The Wong family
third and fourth
generations.

▲► Milton carrying
the 2010 Winter
Olympic torch in
Campbell River,
B.C.

A fantastic chef, Milton was often found in the heart of his home, the
kitchen. He was known for hosting memorable meals and for teaching
married friends to make apple pie to help keep the spark of romance alive.
Milton and Fei's annual Christmas Eve party was legendary, with guests
numbering in the hundreds. Equally famous was the New Year's Day feast
they organized for their extended family, a tradition begun by Milton's
father, which included Chinese delicacies such as roast duck and stewed
pork belly.

Milton inherited his father's interest in the stock market, and throughout his professional career, he showed remarkable business acumen
combined with a strong sense of social responsibility. After graduating
from the University of British Columbia with a degree in political science
and economics, he began his distinguished career at National Trustco
Inc. before founding the investment management firm M.K. Wong and
Associates in 1980. Within six years, Milton's intellectual energy and
entrepreneurial knack had turned M.K. Wong into the second-largest
pension fund firm in B.C. He continued with the company until it was
absorbed and recreated into HSBC Global Asset Management in 1996.
Milton was co-founder of the portfolio management program at UBC's

Sauder School of Business, where he became an inspirational mentor for a generation of young entrepreneurs.

Milton's vision of a Canada where people of all cultures can thrive led him to co-found the Laurier Institution. He served as chancellor of Simon Fraser University from 1999 to 2005. Over the years, he was instrumental in raising funds for and supporting organizations such as the B.C. Cancer Foundation, Vancouver General Hospital, the Red Cross, the Salvation Army, Science World and the YWCA. He played a major role in moving forward many First Nations initiatives and helped to structure land claim and business partnerships for groups across B.C., in particular the Nisga'a Treaty. Together with Fei, Milton was a tireless supporter of the arts, and he helped with the plan to move the SFU School for the Contemporary Arts to the redeveloped Woodward's complex.

Because of his love of cultivating new ideas, Milton was energized by young people. He gave guidance and helped countless people find their

▲◄ Graduation from the University of British Columbia with a political science and economics degree in 1963.

▲ The first production at the Fei and Milton Wong Experimental Theatre at SFU Woodward's was Robert Lepage's *The Blue Dragon*. Milton, Fei and daughter Andrea.

CITY OF VANCOUVER
PROVINCE OF BRITISH COLUMBIA

BY RESOLUTION *of the Council of the City of Vancouver passed on the 12th day of July, in the 59th year of the reign of Her Majesty Queen Elizabeth II and in the year of our Lord, Two Thousand and Eleven, His Worship Mayor Gregor Robertson presiding.*

Freedom of
the City of Vancouver

IS HEREBY BESTOWED UPON
Milton K. Wong

Milton K. Wong was born in Vancouver in 1939, the son of Wong Kung Lai and Chu Man Ming. He was raised in Chinatown alongside his eight siblings and he attended Vancouver public schools.

He has remained devoted to his roots and his achievements as a true city-builder have helped to shape Vancouver into one of the most diverse, vibrant and innovative cities in the world.

He has made tremendous contributions to Vancouver across a wide spectrum of accomplishments in the fields of finance, entrepreneurship, arts and culture, sustainability, volunteerism, community development, multiculturalism, academia and philanthropy.

Throughout his professional career he has shown remarkable business acumen combined with a strong sense of social responsibility. He has spent a lifetime channeling his intellectual energy and entrepreneurial skill into building companies and institutions concerned with the well-being of people.

Above all, he has demonstrated a deep commitment to community service and his influence can be seen across a vast array of successful endeavors that have touched the lives of countless Vancouver residents.

He serves as an inspiration to many for his leadership and compassion.

THEREFORE *Milton K. Wong is hereby entitled to the Freedom of the City.*

In attestation whereof the Seal of the City of Vancouver is hereunto affixed

MAYOR

CITY CLERK

Milton was presented with the Freedom of the City Award, the City of Vancouver's highest and most prestigious award, by Mayor Gregor Robertson in July 2011 among family at Queen Elizabeth Park.

passions. His relationships and conversations with others were what interested him most of all.

Among his many honours, Milton received the Order of Canada, the Order of British Columbia and the City of Vancouver's highest honour, the Freedom of the City Award. Above all, Milton never forgot his roots, and he demonstrated a deep commitment to community service. His influence can be seen in a vast array of successful endeavours that have touched the lives of countless Canadians. He will continue to serve as an inspiration to many for his legacy of leadership and compassion.

▲▲ Celebrating the Freedom of the City Award with friends and family.

▲◀ Mayor Gregor Robertson presenting the Freedom of the City Award.

▲ Fei and Milton.

ONE

Connect the Dots

An original collage from Fei Disbrow, Fei's
goddaughter, given as a birthday gift to Fei.

Untitled
FEI DISBROW | 2009

Conversations
on Culture

MILTON WONG AND I were born in the same year, and we lived most of our lives in the same city, yet we didn't have more than a passing acquaintance until we were in our mid-fifties. Do I regret that now, or do I see it as a necessary progression towards the meeting that really initiated our friendship? I hover. We had both been on a lifelong journey to discover what interested and motivated us most. Perhaps we needed to wait until we had reached a tentative conclusion or two before we were ready to talk.

The first time we had a serious conversation was in the spring of 1995, when I interviewed Milton for a series of profiles of leading community thinkers I was writing for the *Vancouver Sun*'s weekend magazine, *Mix*. He was probably best known then as an investment advisor—"the maestro of money," *BC Business* called him—and he had just been elected chancellor of Simon Fraser University. He had also been involved in launching a number of social and cultural ventures—Science World and the Dragon Boat Festival, for instance—and the editor of *Mix* was intrigued by comments Milton had been making about the changing demographics of Vancouver and Canada.

At the time I interviewed Milton, I was coming to the end of a newspaper career as a writer and commentator about arts and culture. I was also in my second three-year term on the board of the Canada Council for the Arts. Given the changing makeup of creative Canada, diversity was an issue that had been more and more in my thoughts. An immigrant myself from one of the so-called dominant cultures, I welcomed the chance to hear the views of the Canadian-born son of an immigrant who didn't speak English when he first arrived in Vancouver. Maybe Milton Wong and I would have useful things to say to each other.

It was as much a conversation as an interview, with each of us prodding the other into thinking more deeply. Milton came at topics from unexpected angles, throwing out ideas that only gradually coalesced into a coherent shape. It was unsettling and provocative. Later, I would recognize that kind of thinking-out-loud, all-over-the-map dot-connecting as one of his principal ways of making sense of the world.

What became clear to me very quickly was the humane dimension of the man. He was insatiably fascinated with cultural and ethnic diversity in modern Canada, and he was voluntarily reinvesting his talents to help advance his ambitions for social harmony and a better world for everyone. In my piece, I quoted a line from an essay Milton had written: "Vibrant political life and a strong society must be grounded in a strong sense of communal membership."

That struck a chord with me: the idea that any individual who wanted a better country should invest time and energy in building it. Soon I would move on from journalism to what some might consider meatier matters— international affairs, cultural policy, even a brief fling in the political arena. Milton would influence me in all those areas and play an important role in my new career as an author and speaker. That first afternoon in 1995, looking over the harbour and the mountains from his office high in the Hongkong Bank of Canada building, was a significant catalyst. By the time it was over, we had the basis of a firm and lasting friendship.

One of my own pet causes has been the relocation of arts and culture from its position on the fringes of society to the heart of modern life. My volunteer work with the Canada Council and, later, as president of the

Canadian Commission for UNESCO gave me the chance to do some serious thinking and writing about arts policy and cultural diplomacy for the federal government. Milt and I talked a lot about that and about the lessons Canada can provide in the peaceful and productive construction of a multiracial society. "How to deal with cultural change," he told me. "That's probably going to become our major export."

At the same time, he drew me into the planning process for the move of SFU's centre for the arts to the new Woodward's location downtown. I had just received an honorary degree from the university, and, as Milt wryly put it, "Nothing is for nothing." Out of my reflection and engagement emerged a manuscript—more of a manifesto, really—about the importance of culture and the imaginative individual to modern life and our complex social structures. I called it *The Defiant Imagination: Why Culture Matters.*

Without Milt's commitment, the book might not have made it beyond manuscript form. He was so enthusiastic about it that he bought several hundred copies for SFU to distribute to business leaders and directors of cultural institutions around the country. His support gave me a springboard into an area where I had always considered myself an outsider—the academy—and an opportunity to travel widely to make the case for change to a broad spectrum of audiences.

That gesture was typical of his generosity and of the strength of his enthusiasms and beliefs. Also typical was his reluctance to have his help publicly acknowledged. He did much of his good by stealth. Still, he took pleasure in the good that he brought about. "How's our book doing?" he would often ask in the months following its publication. Today, years later, "our book" it will always be.

Max Wyman is a Vancouver writer and arts policy consultant and one of Canada's leading cultural commentators. He was a board member of the Canada Council for the Arts (1996–2002) and president of the Canadian Commission for UNESCO (2002–06). He is an Officer of the Order of Canada and holds an honorary DLitt from Simon Fraser University.

90/230   HAIDA FROG   WALKER BROWN 04

Haida Frog

WALKER BROWN | 2004

Making Things Happen

MILTON WONG FIRST reached out to me sometime in the 1990s, when he invited me to be a guest speaker at the Laurier Institution. I can't recall whether he had seen me on the news discussing a poll or had come across my first book, *Sex in the Snow*. Either way, he must have heard me telling the story of evolving Canadian values and attitudes, a story of Canadians moving from fearing the other to tolerating the other to—among those at the leading edge of social change—savouring the other: embracing diversity as an opportunity for learning, creativity and pleasure.

Milt was one of the visionaries who, early on, glimpsed the power and potential of social diversity in Canada, especially in our cities. Our findings that Canadians were beginning to see diversity as an asset rather than a liability must have pleased him greatly. Openness to social diversity was not unique to Canada, but it was becoming a part of our collective identity in a way that was new. I believe this trend excited Milt partly because he was a tremendously open and curious person, partly because he was the son of immigrants to Canada and maybe above all because he loved to make things happen. Milt made things happen not just by planning and executing them himself but by catalyzing, nudging, coaxing, provoking and challenging them to happen. A country in which one in five people is foreign-born, where big cities are home to dozens of languages and cultural groups and where the average person feels good about—not threatened by—these conditions is a wonderful place to make interesting things happen.

When Milt asked me to address the Laurier Institution, I thought the trip to Vancouver would be an excellent chance for me to have a meal at one of

MILT *made things happen not just by planning and executing them himself but by catalyzing, nudging, coaxing, provoking and challenging them to happen.*

the city's high-end restaurants. But Milt had something more interesting in mind: he gave me a personal tour of Chinatown and a delicious dinner there with some of his many friends. During the tour, he pointed out a couple of windows above a little shop: his old apartment. Milt worked his way to immense success from a modest background, and he undoubtedly encountered racist discrimination along the way. But during our walk through Chinatown and our discussions of his past, he evinced no resentment about this. As on so many topics, he was matter-of-fact and pragmatic to a degree that almost belied his huge imagination and idealism. He preferred to make things happen rather than talk about why they hadn't happened yet.

Milt also tended to be matter-of-fact about his many insights and his constant learning: "You should read this." "You should look into that." "This is worth doing; that is not." Perhaps this simplicity of expression came from a quiet confidence born of making his way so successfully, and plainly under his own steam, in a then less-than-cosmopolitan Canada. He said his piece simply, without a sales pitch; whether you acted on his valuable words was in your court.

One of the things about which Milt proclaimed, matter-of-factly, "This should happen"—and on which, thankfully, I followed his advice—was a project I approached him about in 2007. I had founded the Environics Institute, a non-profit entity that does relevant and original survey research on issues of public importance, and I was considering initiating a survey of Aboriginal people living in Canada's cities. The census had shown that a slight majority of Aboriginal people were living in urban areas. At the time, the mainstream image of Aboriginal people was not only one-dimensional and frequently negative; it was rural, northern, distant from the neighbourhoods of much of the heavily urban Canadian population. And yet more than half a million First Nations, Metis and Inuit people were living in Canadian cities. What did they have to say about their experiences, attitudes, values and aspirations?

I knew this study would be an immense challenge, and I sought as much wise counsel as I could. Naturally, I wanted to hear from Milt. I headed west with my thirteen-year-old son, Will, to seek Milt's thoughts on whether and how to approach this project, the most daunting of my career but also potentially the most significant. In quintessential Milt fashion, he told me two things. Yes, I should do it. As for how, I should hire an exceptional young Nisga'a woman named Ginger Gosnell-Myers to manage the project. And he said something else at that meeting. I needed to do more than hire Ginger; I also needed to stay out of her way. "Listen to her and let her lead," he said simply. We had a competitive national hiring process, but Ginger stood out, as Milt knew she would. I did my best to execute his wise instructions: the Urban Aboriginal Peoples Study (UAPS) went ahead under her excellent leadership, and I am certain it would have faltered without her.

Ginger, as Milt must have known, has an exceptional talent for just the kind of respectful, collaborative leadership at which Milt himself was so skilled. The questions for the study were framed by Aboriginal people, the interviews were conducted largely by Aboriginal people, the project was led at the city level by mostly Aboriginal coordinators, the data were coded by an Aboriginal-owned research firm and the interpretation was done with an advisory circle of largely Aboriginal experts and leaders. In all, the study was completed by a group—call it a network, a team, a community—of hundreds of people. It took a lot of time and thought to build this model and to attract people to participate. It was a journey of creative collaboration for which there was no map. But there was a guide: the philosophy of

Milton K. Wong. Since then, many people—participants in the survey and others—have told me that the UAPS data will be the foundation for future research, policy work, investment and dialogue. As Milt knew well when he encouraged me to embark on the project, gathering data is never the end of the process; it is just the beginning, a tool you then hand off to others so that they can start their own work.

Milt was a great beginner. By that, I mean that he was good at seeing and sparking the beginnings of things that were worthwhile and important. And he managed to maintain his curiosity and openness over his long career, holding on to a beginner's outlook. Milt named his Laurier Institution after former prime minister Wilfrid Laurier, who famously declared that the twentieth century would be Canada's. Laurier sensed he was at the dawn of an exciting, momentous time for his country. Milt Wong's career was marked by a similarly grand sense of possibility. With great deftness and wisdom, he laid the foundations for others—newcomers, Aboriginal peoples, women pursuing business careers, young people, all Canadians—to make their individual, collective, shared and overlapping possibilities real.

Michael Adams *is the founding president of the Environics group of marketing research and communications consulting companies and president of the Environics Institute for survey research. He knew and admired Milton Wong for more than two decades.*

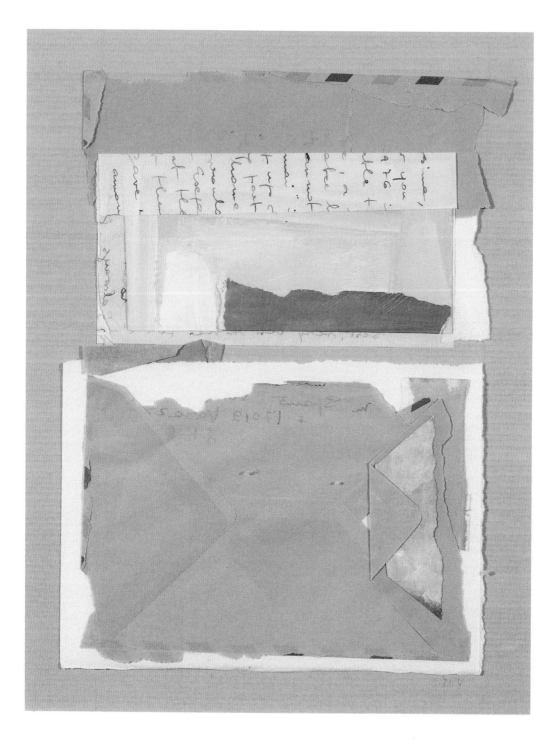

Mixed-media piece by New York artist
Susan Boynton, partner to Milton's business associate.

Port Angelica ɪ and Port Angelica ɪɪ
SUSAN BOYNTON | 1983

A Great Statesman

MET MILT WHEN I was at the University of British Columbia in the Faculty of Commerce. I was a student in the portfolio management program. Milt was one of the founders of the program, which gave students the chance to manage a real-life portfolio of stocks and bonds. There were six of us, and Milt took us all under his wing. I remember we went to Milt's office and he said: "Hi, I'm Milt. Don't call me Mr. Wong, call me Milt. If you call me Mr. Wong we can never be friends, because we are in a superior-inferior relationship."

He believed there was a need for future fund managers to have more hands-on training, including a networking component and leadership about how to behave. Giving back to the community was a big part of it, Milt told us, because everything grows together accordingly. And knowing the people side of finance is really important, because it's not just analytics; it's about ethics and modes of behaviour. If you think about all the things you hear about Wall Street, it gets down to this: you have to have a core set of beliefs and strong values. Milt was trying to inject that into the portfolio management program.

Our team got half a million dollars to manage among six somewhat cocky students. To make an investment, you need five of the six students to agree. You also have a client committee to whom you present your investments, as if they are your client and you are managing their money. You get a couple of mentors too, so there is a lot of real-world learning.

Everything forces you to learn to be better prepared, a lot sharper. At our first client committee meeting, we just wrote up our report and went in—we thought it was going to be great. Then the client committee, all these experienced investors who were running funds, started grilling us with questions. "Why did you invest in that?" "You say this, but your outlook really says this instead." Yeah... "Well, you invested in this, but you said that. That fund's leverage is based on the Canadian dollar going up. This one's based on the Canadian dollar going down when you really get down to it."

We walked out of there, the six of us, and I think we were in tears. None of us had ever failed at anything before. But all of a sudden, we just looked stupid. There were inconsistencies in our investments that we didn't even know. That was a year of the most humbling experiences you can imagine.

By now, probably 150 people have passed through the UBC portfolio management program. It's existed for twenty-five years. It's not that many students, but they are now in some pretty senior positions throughout the investment industry, which is exactly what Milt was hoping for. It's had an impact in Vancouver, Toronto and New York.

I think most of the portfolio management graduates, who have had the foundation of the program, understand that if you are doing well, you should give back. If you've gotten somewhere yourself, you remember you got there because somebody else created that program. So you need to decide what you believe in and how you can help make the future better.

After I graduated, I went to Chrysler Canada to help manage their pension fund and corporate cash. I did my two years and decided I couldn't live in Windsor. After talking to Milt a few times, I decided to move back to Vancouver to join Distinctive Software. Two years later, we became part of Electronic Arts. During those years, Milt provided great advice on what we should be doing at Distinctive Software. He introduced me to a lot of people. He kept inviting me to charity dinners, and he went to many of them. I was really shy, and it was at least three years before I stopped feeling really intimidated by all these business people. After a while, you start thinking, "Hey, I actually know this guy, because I've seen him eight times." Milt was a big part of who I am, in helping me to break out and get connected to the business community and in encouraging me to become involved in the community in general.

Having Milt as a mentor built my understanding. I spent a lot of time watching him, learning from him, basically analyzing him and watching how people responded to him. We had a lot of great conversations about it. What I do now, at Vanedge Capital, is based on the same concept of talking to as many people as possible, building a strong network, and then finding a way to make something happen. Milt was phenomenal at making things happen.

Milt had such a strong value system. Over time you realize, if you really want to do something, there are going to be pressures. You need a strong value system to guide what you will do and what you won't. Fast money is not always the best money. A company also needs a strong value system and a strong culture that defines it. If your employees don't understand what your company is all about and why, if they don't realize you're all on a mission to build something for a shared cause, then you're going to get a lot of temporary employees who aren't going to work that hard and are just working there for the money.

Milt was very self-aware. He focussed on his own areas of expertise and got people who specialized in other areas to work for him. He was the type who was always out there meeting people too, and as a result he had better information about major trends and the global economy. I learned from Milt that you first have to understand the major trends. Then you can invest with the rising tide as opposed to a falling tide.

After we sold Distinctive Software, Milt said, "Look, I'm really buried in this company called ALI Technologies. You understand the space, so I want you to come in and invest some money and help figure out what needs to be done." ALI at the time was developing new technologies in breast cancer screening, but it was not working, and the company needed to pivot. Milt's wife, Fei, had recovered from breast cancer awhile earlier, so he was personally very committed to ALI. We eventually sold it to McKesson Corp. for $530 million.

When I turned forty, Milt came to me and said, "Hey, you know what? This is it. Now or never. I was forty when I made the decision to start M.K. Wong. You're forty now, and you've got to do something on your own. What do you believe in?" It took a few years, but I got my butt in gear and started this venture capital fund called Vanedge Capital.

What gets me up in the morning is building something. If we can get good returns on our first fund, then there will be a second fund, and there will be a third fund. We can build ourselves into a top-tier venture fund. There are no recognized top-tier technology venture funds in Canada now, and we need one. Vancouver's never really going to be a global city, or Canada a global leader, if we don't have any global technology companies headquartered here. And it's a chicken-and-egg thing. It takes one major successful company to get it started, and so we hope that by raising this fund we will get one. It's taking a long-term view, building something that we hope will allow the whole ecosystem to change here. I am sure Milt, and M.K. Wong, gave up a lot of dollars in investment because he wouldn't move to Toronto. But he wanted to build the ecosystem here in Vancouver

I remember a conversation in which Milt offered some real insight. He said, "Look, here's what's happening. I'm doing all this stuff, like the Dragon Boat Festival, Science World, etc. When things are going well at M.K. Wong, they tell me I'm a great guy because I'm doing all this stuff. When things aren't going well at M.K. Wong, they say I'm an idiot because I'm doing all this stuff and not focussing on M.K. Wong. How you're doing matters more to a lot of people than what you're doing. But I'm doing this because I want to do it and I believe in it."

Milt was a great spokesman. He was a fantastic networker. You could bring any type of person to meet Milt, and they liked talking to him. He was totally open. Those are enormous qualities. Because that wasn't what he cared about, I'm not even sure he was that great an investor. But he was a man of integrity, he was a great statesman, and he was a great person.

Paul Lee *was a director of* ALI *Technologies, past president of Electronic Arts, a managing partner of Vanedge Capital and a mentee, friend and business partner.*

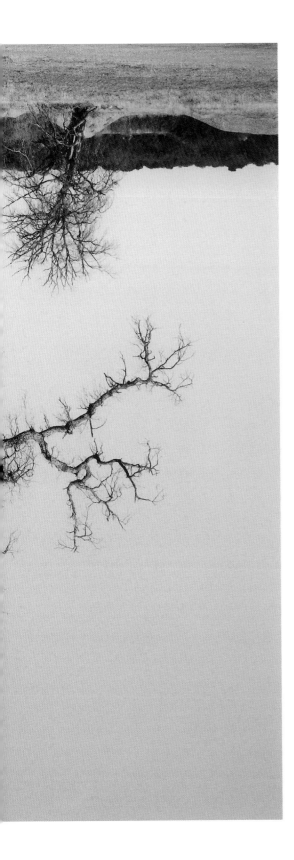

Acquired after Fei and Milton had completed the construction of the family's residence at the Taku resort on Quadra Island. The tree feature of the family residence was partly inspired by this Rodney Graham photograph, which was also meant to highlight the living roof. Milton and Fei were both passionate protectors of B.C.'s coastal wilderness. The Wongs have transformed Taku into a place for escape, for families, and for authentic outdoor adventures that inspire a connection with and stewardship of B.C.'s wilderness. At Taku, Milton hosted community workshops, courses, and opportunities for the community to connect. Named after a Tlingit word, "Taku" roughly translates to a feeling of peace and togetherness at the nesting sites of birds. Fittingly, Taku became an informal location for gathering inspired minds and leaders to imagine the future of Canada.

Oak Tree, Red Bluff #8
RODNEY GRAHAM | 1993/2005

Crystallizing
Synergies

FIRST MET MILTON WONG through our mutual friend Brian DeBeck in the
late 1990s. The three of us went for wontons at the Ho Tak Kee and talked
about the new wave of Chinese art, just then emerging on the world stage.

Soon after, Milton toured me through the sprawling downtown offices
of M.K. Wong and Associates, which looked like an art gallery. The walls
were covered with the silkscreen prints of his sister Anna, who had studied
at the Art Students League in New York and taught printmaking for
many years at the Vancouver School of Art, now Emily Carr University
of Art + Design. Milton shared his family's creative spirit and love for art.
I learned only much later that I had already met his mother-in-law, Sue Gee
Jackman, who ran the Kuo Kong Silk Company. At one point, Sue had shared
a space at Pender and Abbott with a man selling local ceramics. It was one
of my favourite haunts at the time. Later, she moved in with Milton's
brothers Bill and Jack at Modernize Tailors, another magical destination.
Bill and Jack once made authentic bebopper zoot suits for artist Eric Metcalfe
and me, which we wore on European tour as the MacBooty Brothers.

Milton went his own way, following a unique genius for finance and
community leadership, but he never forgot his Chinatown roots, and
he retained a deep respect for the land and its Aboriginal heritage. This,
combined with his boundless curiosity and authentic compassion, made him
a living treasure to his nation and an inspiring example to his peers.

Among his many contributions to educational, scientific and cultural
initiatives (Milton Wong was a one-man UNESCO), he was a co-founder of

Centre A in 1999, along with Zheng Shengtian, Stephanie Holmquist, Jin Me Yoon and me. Milton had already helped with the production of our pilot project, a city-wide exhibition of contemporary Chinese art. I remember him listening attentively at the Jiangnan symposium and spontaneously, as he so often did, hosting a number of the speakers at dim sum afterwards. Centre A, short for the Vancouver International Centre for Contemporary Asian Art, is a multi-faceted art gallery that is still going strong today. Between 2000 and 2012, Centre A produced 97 exhibition projects representing the work of 426 Canadian and international artists, as well as numerous symposia, performances, concerts and community outreach collaborations. Milton remained a constant supporter and promoter of Centre A, often helping to build the board and make connections.

Milton had a knack for surprising you at key moments with a gift or an introduction. He loved nothing more than to put people together, crystallizing synergies that could snowball into city-changing innovations. He was a true patron of Centre A. Without being asked, he called up more than once to announce a crucial donation, seeming to sense when this gesture would most be needed. He would sometimes drop by the gallery with interesting people on his arm, suggesting a new collaboration. In this way, he connected Centre A to social housing initiatives on the Downtown Eastside and mentored a collaboration with the Aga Khan Foundation to examine the ways that arts and culture can contribute to the renaissance of historic but neglected inner-city neighbourhoods.

Over the years, I became friends with Milton and his wife, Fei. When Milton was on the road, Fei and I would occasionally go out to fundraisers together. This was a special treat for me. Once Milton called out of the blue to say that he'd ordered a suit for me at Modernize and that I should go over to the shop to get myself measured. Typical Milton!

The last time I saw Milton was about a year before he died, at a small but spectacular dinner in Shanghai hosted by another visionary patron of the arts, Yu Yu. The guest list included Kathleen Bartels, director of the Vancouver Art Gallery, and renowned clothing designer Lin Li of JNBY. The conversation at dinner turned to the idea of creating a major institution for contemporary Asian art in Vancouver. This was just the kind of concept that appealed to Milton. He understood exactly the urgency and meaning of such an idea. At the end of the dinner, we all rose to toast the vision, resolving to meet again at the opening of the new centre. On the day when that happens, I know Milton will be with us.

Hank Bull *is an artist and arts administrator. He worked closely with Milton Wong on the creation of Centre A, the Vancouver International Centre for Contemporary Asian Art.*

Radical Stewardship

MANY WILL REMEMBER Milton Wong, business leader and philanthropist, for his inspiring legacy of social contributions, which touched countless hearts and communities across Canada.

I will remember my uncle for his typically cheeky response to any new challenge: "Well, what are you going to do about it?"

For Milton, no matter how insurmountable the problem, there was a way to step forward. He loved to grow outrageously big ideas and impossible dreams.

Milton found early success as an investor in finance, but he was more accurately an investor in possibility. From start-ups to new festivals to public projects, his passion for nourishing innovation was infectious. At times, Milton's interests seemed wildly diverse and even unrelated—the arts, multiculturalism, social justice. But for him, everything was easily unified under one single concept: stewardship.

It's a word I first heard as a child, when adults talked about cleaning up streams or protecting salmon. A word for a sign on a forest trail, wooden and old-fashioned.

But although my uncle considered himself an environmentalist, stewardship to him wasn't just about protecting the natural world. It was about the deeper well-being of people, culture and democracy. Milton's vision of stewardship imagined a radically hopeful planet. Its definition was simple: Stewardship is the act of caring for that which does not belong to you. For my uncle, everything and everyone was deserving of safety: a new immigrant, an endangered rainforest, a Nisga'a oral tradition or a struggling women's shelter.

In the spring of 2011, Milton came to visit me in China, where I've worked in the environmental sector for the last five years. Although Milton's childhood Chinese vocabulary was limited to subjects like dim sum, he still thrived in China, where the impact of good ideas immediately went to scale. As we walked together under coal-stained skies in the polluted chaos of Beijing, Milton spoke of the urgency facing our interconnected planet and the importance of reaching out across cultures: "China is where the world's story is happening, kid. You can't come home yet."

Everyone, Milton felt, has the right to what he most cherished: watching the tides wash over rocky coastal beaches, digging through wet sand for clams with your children, waking to a golden dawn poured over cedar trees. He was passionate about a borderless stewardship, one that calls us to open our hearts to the lives of people thousands of miles away.

As naturalist John Muir wrote: "When we try to pick out anything by itself, we find that it is bound fast by a thousand invisible cords that cannot be broken, to everything in the universe."

The world that my uncle imagined asks us to take the idea of stewardship off the sign on a forest trail and into our lives and relationships. To care for that which does not belong to us. It asks us, no matter how immense the challenge, to take a step forward. Towards the planet, towards each other and towards possibility.

Joanna Wong is a principal at Flow Creative, a creative agency that specializes in marketing in China. Her passions for sustainability, big ideas and family dinners were inspired by her uncle Milton.

MILTON K. WONG
A Global Civil Society

PUBLISHED IN
THE *VANCOUVER SUN*, APRIL 2, 2008

BELIEVE INTUITIVELY THAT the notion of a civil society hinges on a finely balanced state of interdependency among all living organisms, such that each is free to optimize its full potential without significantly infringing on another's ability to do the same.

If I had just forty words to tell you what I think is meant by the term "civil society," that's what it would all come down to for me.

It's a lofty mouthful, I know, and it doesn't come with a neat sidebar of practical suggestions for how we can achieve this perfect balance. But I believe that to talk of practicalities, first we need a philosophical framework that will give us the common language required to assess our society and find out what needs changing. And a central part of that framework, for me, is the tenet that all living beings should enjoy the opportunity to live the most meaningful lives possible—whatever that actually means for each particular creature.

Clearly, we're not there yet. We need only look at how we treat our homeless people, our Aboriginal people and many other disenfranchised groups in our society to see that some of us are exploring every avenue of our potential while others are spending their entire lives behind the starting line. You could take this line of reasoning further and consider the way we commonly mistreat animals (for example, on industrial farms) or indeed the planet itself, assaulting it with chemicals and toxins, destroying old-growth forests and spewing massive quantities of greenhouse gases into the atmosphere. We have done a spectacular job of ensuring that mainly humans, and only the strongest, enjoy the luxury of optimizing their existence on earth.

To understand how we can return to a more sustainable path and a truly civil society, first we need to understand how we got ourselves into this mess in the first place. It seems to me that the answer can be found in John Ralston Saul's book *Voltaire's Bastards: The Dictatorship of Reason in the West*. Saul reminds us that the central idea during the Age of Reason was that since people could reason, think and invent to suit themselves—but animals could not—people must be superior to all living creatures, free to assert their dominion over the earth without regard to consequences.

That was bad enough—but as a society, we took it a step further and applied that notion to different groups of people, viewing some as more human than others. Chinese or Aboriginal people, for example, were seen as less human. The Age of Reason also ushered in the era of colonialism, a major contributor to the economic disparities we still see today between the developed and the developing worlds.

The notion of social democracy arose in the Commonwealth only after the Age of Reason—after industrialization and colonialism. Because the social framework came second, we're still suffering the consequences of that winner-takes-all age.

Obviously, there are many wrongs that still need to be set right. To our credit, we have been moving (albeit slowly) in that direction since the Universal Declaration of Human Rights some sixty years ago. From basic human rights to gender rights, gay rights, Aboriginal rights and, more recently, the right to clean air and nutrition, as a global society we have been progressing steadily towards a world where internationally recognized rights transcend national sovereign borders.

The ongoing challenge is: How do you get diverse countries, cultures and segments of society to commit voluntarily to a shared set of values? As Canadians, we know very well how difficult it can be to balance collective rights with individual ones. We've experienced it with the prospect of a separate Quebec, with Aboriginal land claims and with the discussion of sharia law in Ontario, to offer just a few examples. But the good news is Canadians seem to have a talent for accommodation. It's been part of our national psyche since Baldwin and LaFontaine in the early nineteenth century, despite some bumps along the way. That's why His Highness the Aga Khan has spent hundreds of millions of dollars building the Centre for Pluralism in Ottawa: he believes this process of accommodation is the key to peace on earth. And I agree with him.

But if it's to happen, then civil society can't be understood as a luxury reserved for those of us who live in developed, democratic countries. Notwithstanding the fact that nations grow at different speeds and have significant cultural differences, I believe the values of a sustainable civil society can be international. I believe it is possible that, some day, we will be able to establish a global system of values to which all countries can adhere without fear of losing their identities. When and if that happens, we will be living in a civil society that is global. We will have understood how to accommodate one another so that people everywhere can optimize their potential as human beings.

Bust through Walls

Milton was drawn to Ed Burtynsky's shipyard
series because of his work with the board of Seaspan
and the inherent commentary on sustainability.

Shipyard #17, Qili Port, Zhejiang Province
EDWARD BURTYNSKY | 2005

We're All Canadian
in the Water

FIRST MET MILT through Science World, in 1983 or '84. I found it very exciting that he was never afraid of a new idea or a new concept. He was intellectually very interesting, because he was always figuring out what was the new thing. I remember sitting with him in about 1988, and he said, "Oh! I Discovered the Internet!" That was at a time when most of us could barely open our cell phones. But he would talk about how he'd been surfing until two in the morning.

So Milt was always the first to look at something new, grasp the importance of it and then get very involved.

The whole idea of a science centre for Vancouver emanated out of a family trip my husband and I took back east. My husband was the person who put Granville Island together, and he wanted to create a market that truly worked. So we went to all the markets. On that trip, we arrived in Toronto with our seven-year-old and nine-year-old sons, and they were bouncing on the bed. So off we went to the Ontario Science Centre. I had never seen a science centre before. Watching them interact and enjoy it, I thought, "Okay, this is what we need in B.C."

After that, every time my husband visited a public market, whether it was in Boston or New York, I went off to the science centre. I decided this was a really critical idea, and I spent three or four years banging around and getting people to join. The breakthrough came when Milt joined our board, because he was a very well-known Vancouver businessman. That sent a real signal to the business community: "Oh! We'd better pay attention!"

What did Milt see? At that point, B.C.'s economy, our strength, was very much the resource industries. One thing Milt saw was that maybe the next generation of businesses would be in high tech, biotech or whatever. But he also understood that most people, when they heard the word "science," were scared, in awe or turned off. He saw the importance of bringing up a generation of people who would say, "Yes! Science could be something I'm interested in." Milt saw that as a future driver of the B.C. economy. And he truly espoused the idea. He'd come to board meetings and he'd know about how many businesses had started because their city had a science centre and about how kids were captured by it. He'd done all his research, and I think that really describes his enthusiasm.

What I loved about Milt was that he didn't flirt. He didn't play. He went right to the core and then figured out "Well, how can we use this? How will it make the province better? Or the country better?" I'm sure half the world thought that he was a kook. But he pulled people together on so many interesting causes. One of those was the Laurier Institution, where I served as vice-chair for many years. It was a think tank that did research on the social and economic impacts of immigration.

In the 1980s, people arriving from Hong Kong were buying up all the properties in Shaughnessy and building, in some cases, absolutely atrocious houses—and, more importantly, building right to the edge of the lot. The streetscape, the landscape was literally changing before people's eyes. So there was a lot of resentment. Milt was concerned about how this was all going to play out, because house prices, of course, went through the roof. He wanted people to make decisions based on proper information. So his first commission through the Laurier Institution was to get to the bottom of what was driving house prices. He would say, "We don't care what the results are. We'll publish them." Not like the Fraser Institute, where you often know what their reports will say. Well, it turned out that what was really driving house prices was an influx of snowbirds trying to escape Manitoba, Alberta and Saskatchewan. There was that whole bulge in the population, and they were buying in at the bottom end.

The Laurier Institution had one and a half staff people. Most of what we did was commission studies on issues such as immigration and First Nations. We made sure the results were properly vetted by peers and that there was no bias. And what was intriguing was that mainstream media was desperately looking for that sort of information. We would get calls from *Maclean's* magazine at least once a month. We'd be quoted.

First Nations issues in the province at the time were being reported very poorly, in an inflammatory way. It was a time when First Nations were pursuing land claims and suggesting that much of B.C. was under negotiation. Milt and I said, "Okay, well, what would be the thing to do here?" We brought in a group of academics to study jobs, land claims and history, and the institution published this as a book called *Prospering Together*.

We arranged a dinner with Matthew Coon Come, who was grand chief of the Assembly of First Nations at the time. The only corporate support we could get was from CN and B.C. Hydro. Every other company's attitude was: "Nope! Not my problem. Don't want to face it. Don't want to deal with it." So we organized this dinner. Milt and I called it the "salt and pepper dinner," because we didn't let all the First Nations people sit at one table and all the white guys sit at another table. We mixed everybody up. There were five hundred people in the room, and I would wager that only twenty of them might have spoken to each other before that night. The dinner was a huge success in that sense. Matthew Coon Come was a great speaker, but more importantly, people started having conversations. That's what it's all about. People have been pigeonholed somewhere, but it turns out that often we have the same values. When I think of Milt, those are the things I think of. It's the same kind of thinking that probably triggered the Dragon Boat Festival. People of all ages and ethnicities were in boats together. Everyone felt Canadian in the water! I give Milt so much credit for connecting the dots.

Milt told me the most creative time in his life was while he was sitting on the Science World board. Why? Because all of a sudden people were literally giving up half their time, part of their daytime jobs, to help move this project forward. It took forever. I thought I'd be dead before it was finished. Some stellar people in the community gave a lot of time and expertise to help me get to where we needed to go. When I first invited Milt to join the board, he was very probing in our discussion. Then, when I started talking about the economy, he said, "Okay. You know what you're doing." In other words, I wasn't some sort of starry-eyed person looking around the room. I understood the economic benefit of what we were trying to do.

Another thing Milt was very keen on was Leadership Vancouver, a program for which I was a co-founder. It was a community leadership training program for people in their thirties and forties, emerging leaders in their areas. It was a not-for-profit undertaking with a cultural overlay. Every class had two or three Ismaili members, two or three Persians, two or three Asian Canadians and folks from the corporate, labour and public sectors. Milt became so enthusiastic he would come to the retreat and be one of the guest speakers, and eventually he became the honorary chair. He understood that the program worked because people had to work together on a project. They all thought they were there to learn leadership skills. Well, that was the hook. What they were really there to learn was: you like to operate a certain way because you're an accountant, and I like to operate a certain way because I'm a lawyer. They learned that their way might not be the best way—or, if it was, they had to bring the whole group along. Because you can't be a great leader if no one is following. Apparently Milt's mother had said that about someone: "Well, if he's such a leader, how come nobody's following him?" It was a story Milt loved to tell.

I adored Milt. I thought he was great. And anytime I could work on a project with him, it was simply "Call me." He was an incredible citizen, in the truest sense of the word.

Barbara Brink *is vice president of Applied Strategies Ltd., a management consulting firm. For several years, she was a provincially appointed public governor of the Vancouver Stock Exchange. She serves on the boards of the Legal Services Society, the B.C. Institute of Chartered Accountants and Junior Achievement of B.C. As president of the board of governors and* CEO, *she was a driving force behind the creation of Vancouver's Science World.*

Acquired at a fundraiser for Simon Fraser

University's newly founded Centre for the

Comparative Study of Muslim Societies

and Cultures, established to encourage

the academic discussion and public

understanding of the cultures and societies

of Muslim peoples.

Friendship in Community

ILTON WONG AND I met as students in a University of British Columbia car pool around 1961. Milton lived in his family's splendid Cambie Street home near West 33rd Avenue. I lived a couple of blocks away in the Queen Elizabeth Park area.

Among the group, Milt stood out as a guy full of life and curiosity, with a deep attachment to his heritage and the Chinese experience on the West Coast. I remember as though it were yesterday when he invited me to his home—so beautifully designed in the West Coast architecture of the time and infused with exquisite Chinese art. Western and Chinese cultures were harmoniously portrayed.

Milton also introduced me to the knowledge that the relationship between Chinese and Anglo Canadians was not always so harmonious. Coming from the dominant Anglo-Saxon culture, I had little appreciation of the head tax imposed on Chinese immigrants, the restrictions on family immigration, the denial of the vote, the discrimination in professional occupations and the withholding of even the right to renovate and expand your own home. (The city's refusal to provide a building permit to Milton's father in Strathcona, because the city had other plans for the area, had resulted in the family's move to Cambie Street.) All of this my ebullient, gentle friend transmitted to me with a quiet intensity that struck me deeply.

Following university, Milt and I both moved to Toronto, Milt for the world of high finance and I to do youth and world affairs education for the United Nations Association in Canada. We didn't see a lot of one another

MILT stood out as a guy full of life and curiosity, with a deep attachment to his heritage and the Chinese experience on the West Coast.

there, though I do recall an enjoyable evening at the Stratford Festival. Years later, we both found ourselves back in Vancouver, married with children. Still, our contact was minimal until 1999, when I became the director of the Carnegie Community Centre at Main and Hastings, near Milt's old family neighbourhood.

At Carnegie, I relished the diverse cultural heritage of Vancouver's Downtown Eastside. I discovered how important arts and culture were to local residents and observed the leading role the Carnegie Centre played in arts programs. The arts, I learned, help people to affirm their identities and give voice and purpose to people's lives and aspirations. The arts also build bridges between different cultures. Importantly, they can be made accessible and affordable to anyone. In short, the arts are a powerful means for personal and community development, especially for people who live at the social and economic margins.

It was in this context that I reconnected with Milt and began a close collaboration that continued until his death. The Carnegie board and staff were planning to celebrate the one-hundredth anniversary of the Carnegie Centre building in 2003. Community arts was the theme—a great way to recognize the area's heritage and what it has contributed to Vancouver. It would also be a great way to bring people together, to remind them and the city as a whole about the considerable strengths in the Downtown Eastside. We saw the celebration as a basis for revitalizing a community that has been unfairly burdened with issues beyond its control.

The year before the celebration, I called Milt and asked if he could lend a hand with some fundraising. He replied that, much as he would like to, he was very committed to other obligations. Six months passed, and we were still looking for someone to lead our anniversary fundraising. In desperation I wrote a letter to Milt, beginning, "This may cost me a good friendship, but..." and asking him to reconsider. Shortly thereafter, I got a phone call from Milt: "Let's meet at the Ovaltine Café and talk."

Prior to the meeting with him, I sought advice about how best to approach Milt. It was suggested that I ask if he knew ten people who could be contacted for $5,000 each, to give us $50,000 to launch the fundraising. So at the Ovaltine, over soup and the usual menu, I broached the subject. Almost before I had finished, Milt said, "I will give you $50,000." I heard it, but I couldn't quite believe it. Besides, I had rehearsed this pitch, so I finished the rest of my mental script. Then I paused and said, "You are serious. You will contribute $50,000 to get us started?" "Yes" was his reply. "I regard it as a social investment."

It turned out to be an investment with excellent social and financial returns. Milt joined a fundraising group chaired by Russ Anthony of Stantec, Dave Mowat of Vancity, then Vancouver mayor Phillip Owen, Milt's colleague Jim Bishop, Leonard Schein of the Schein Foundation, Don Shumka of Walden Financial Management and Margaret Prevost and Peter Fairchild, president and treasurer respectively of the Carnegie Community Centre Association. Over the next two years, this group helped raise more than $1 million for the community arts in the DTES and the Carnegie anniversary.

It wasn't only the financial connections these great people had that were made available to us. Again, through Milt's initiative and that of others, we benefited from the mentoring these friends of Carnegie provided or arranged for Carnegie staff and community members in the organization of our major anniversary events. Our community classroom topics were working with the media, finances, record-keeping, planning and registration procedures. Finally, these deeply committed civic leaders became ambassadors to the city at large for the Downtown Eastside. They took to their own constituencies the message that amidst the apparent desperation of the Downtown Eastside there was hope and that talent and strength to forge a healthy future resided among those who lived there.

The social returns were many. During that twelve-month period, we held a community historic markers walk, a spring cherry blossom celebration, a DTES film festival and a horse-drawn buggy and community parade down Hastings Street from Victory Square to Main and Hastings, with music, food and more. The highlight was the first-ever DTES Community Play, *In the Heart of the City,* produced by Vancouver Moving Theatre. More than any other event, this project epitomized the power of the arts for personal and community development. The early stages involved seven months of community workshops and tea parties to collect people's stories about the Downtown Eastside, plus research into the area's rich history. Then there were open auditions: everyone who wanted a part in the play was accepted, whether as an actor, a musician, a costume maker or a set designer. Professional theatre people mentored each component. The result was a resounding success: six sold-out three-hundred-seat performances over two weeks at the Japanese Hall in the DTES.

All of this took the community arts in the DTES to a whole new level. Since then, there has been a community opera, a musical based on the Bruce Erickson–Libby Davies story, a shadow puppet production on addictions and more. The Heart of the City Festival is now in its ninth year, produced by Vancouver Moving Theatre in association with the Carnegie Community Centre, the Association of United Ukrainian Canadians and a host of other DTES partners.

What does all this mean? It means that, each year, literally hundreds of community residents are engaged in community arts. It means that forty-plus local organizations are now collaborating on arts projects. It means that new skills and knowledge are being acquired and old skills polished up. And it means building collective community pride and changing perceptions about the Downtown Eastside, with annual audiences for the festival in the seven-to-eight-thousand range.

Perhaps it is most fittingly expressed in the words of former Vancouver city councillor Ellen Woodsworth: "In all the years I've worked in the DTES, nothing has transformed people in the community as much as the Heart of the City Festival." Or this, from Peter Birnie of the *Vancouver Sun:* "The Heart of the City Festival reminds Vancouver that for every negative aspect of life at our core, proof of a dynamic community working hard to deal with its problems is also very much in evidence." After attending the launch of the seventh annual festival in October 2010, Lieutenant-Governor Steven Point arranged for the Carnegie Jazz Band to perform to great acclaim at Government House in Victoria the following summer. Not a bad return on a $50,000 social investment.

There is a sequel to this story, again stemming directly from Milton Wong. In 2005, the friends of Carnegie realized that gentrification was an increasing threat to the area and that the low-income residents, who had demonstrated so much resilience to maintain their community—and for whom community arts had become such a powerful tool, giving voice to their stories and their dreams—were at risk of losing that community.

Milt said that something had to be done. Neither he nor the other friends were interested in contributing time and money to a gentrified community. This time it was his turn to call on me. He asked me to convene a meeting of local residents, business people and community workers. We did so in September 2005, and Milton presented the idea of these groups coming together to create a common "social compact" for the DTES—a framework to guide development that would ensure the neighbourhood would remain a home for people with low incomes, with the requisite housing, cohesive services, education, training and job opportunities—and of course with the arts in a central role.

Subsequently, we formed the Building Community Society (BCS) to act as a resource and facilitator to the process, to demonstrate how the social compact could work and to advocate for a comprehensive planning approach to the DTES. Milton was the first chair of the society and typically lent his time, his talents and his ideas to this work, as well as provided significant funding personally and arm-twisted others. The ensuing years were intense and demanding. BCS assembled a group from the public and private sectors: planners, facilitators, architects, financial and business people, non-profit administrators and community workers—fifteen in total to contribute, pro bono, their time and experience in the cause of community renewal in the Downtown Eastside. The work has been immensely challenging, given all of the parties and interests involved. There were times when it felt like nothing was going to emerge, despite the time, the effort and the funds invested.

Now, in the winter of 2012/13, it can be reported that:

BCS joined with Builders Without Borders to provide planning, management and financial assistance to the Aboriginal Mother Centre Society, which opened earlier this year. It is a unique, purpose-built residential and drop-in facility with services for Aboriginal mothers and their newborns.

BCS is also co-chairing, with the Downtown Eastside Neighbourhood Council, a local area planning committee established by the city in 2011. The committee, composed of local residents (a majority of whom live on low incomes) and local business associations, is working on a comprehensive plan for the whole Downtown Eastside. A priority is to ensure that there will be safe, affordable housing for low-income residents and that people will continue to feel the DTES is their "home."

Milton Wong's relentless optimism, his remarkable creativity as an ideas person, his vast networks and his abilities at matchmaking provided the foundation for all the achievements that have been reported here. Combine that with his deep belief in the importance of helping people learn for themselves and in building bridges of understanding and collaboration across interests and cultures, and you have a powerful formula for positive social change.

Rick Lam, then chair of the Chinatown Revitalization Committee, expressed these convictions eloquently when presenting a cheque for $18,000 to the Carnegie Centre for building community capacity through the arts in 2005: "Carnegie is often referred to as the Heart of the Community. My dream and my goal is that with Chinatown, Carnegie and all the communities in the area working together, someday the whole Downtown Eastside will be referred to as the heart and soul of Vancouver. I think we can do it. United, we can."

Michael Clague's career in community work and social policy has included the three levels of government and the voluntary sector. He was the director of the Carnegie Community Centre from 1999 to 2005. In 2008, he received the Order of Canada.

An early piece by Gordon Smith.
Purchased from the Equinox Gallery.

Aspects of the Harbour

GORDON SMITH | 1960

Finding Common Ground in the Historic District

THOSE OF US who were around Milton Wong for some time witnessed the genesis of his passion and vision. While still at university, he would convene extracurricular sessions to discuss how the world could become a better place. Typical, perhaps, for a young aspiring activist. What wasn't typical were the many ventures that Milton went on to initiate. It is safe to say that this "talker" grew into an incredibly accomplished "doer."

Milton's many innovative projects are well known. He excelled at bringing the appropriate people and ideas together with his articulate passion and vision. Once those people were engaged, he would leave them to do their job, with his tacit support. With this kind of approach, he would then be free to carry out more initiatives.

My own involvement included the Centre for Contemporary Asian Art—Centre A—of which Milton was a champion and supporter. In 2006, seeing the lack of progress in improving the quality of life for people in the Downtown Eastside despite many government programs, Milton launched a gathering with the goal of bringing a common ground of conduct to the area. He convened this meeting of about fifty people with diverse and sometimes opposing points of view to arrive at a "social compact" on how things could be done. His idea was to model the conflict resolution approach that had been used successfully by the Aga Khan Foundation in different parts of the world.

A year later, Milton formed a group eventually called the Building Community Society of Greater Vancouver. BCS became an advocate and facilitator for the Downtown Eastside and homelessness issues. The group was composed of about a dozen volunteer professionals, myself included, and three part-time staff members. In the early years, BCS was influential in assisting important projects such as the First United Church community project and the Aboriginal Mother Centre Society. After BCS had pursued the city for three years to develop a local area plan for the Downtown Eastside, the city asked the society to co-chair the initial preparations with the Downtown Eastside Neighbourhood Council. This was a very ambitious initiative in an extremely complex political environment.

Another project I worked on with Milton was a little more personal and unusual. Although he kept saying that he was "not a developer," he set out to restore the Chinese Freemasons Building at 5 West Pender Street. The building had been the headquarters for the Chinese Freemasons when they hosted Dr. Sun Yat-sen, the leading revolutionary for a republican China, in Vancouver in 1911. Milton's father started Modernize Tailors on the ground floor of the building in 1913. Milton and his brother Maurice had played in the shop while their older brothers, Bill and Jack, worked alongside their father. Shortly after World War II, the business was forced to move across the street.

Bill and Jack carried on the family business, and they were thrilled to return Modernize Tailors to its original location in 2008, when the building was fully restored. Milton had also bought the building with the intention of providing rental accommodation to people who wanted to return to Chinatown, their childhood environment. In that way, this fine historic building contributed to the Chinatown revitalization program during a critical period for the area. As such projects invariably encounter complex city and federal red tape, Milton entrusted his daughter Elizabeth to oversee the proceedings.

The stories of Modernize Tailors and of Chinatown between 1901 and 1911 contributed an added level of significance to the building. These stories, curated by the Chinese Canadian Historical Society and edited by Milton's niece, Joanna Wong, are on display today in the glass windows of the ground floor—just like the newspaper pages of the *Chinese Times* were one hundred years ago. I feel privileged to have been a part of this endeavour, with its many layers of historic and personal significance to the Wong family and to Vancouver's Chinatown. The project has been recognized by Heritage B.C., the Vancouver Heritage Commission and the Architectural Institute of B.C.

Joe Wai, *architect, AIBC, FRAIC, DLitt, became friends with Milton and Maurice Wong while the three of them were in high school.*

The Meaning
of Inclusivity

THE WORD "INCLUSIVE" is one that I learned from Milton Wong. Or not the word, exactly, but the concept. It has helped to define many things in my life and the many projects that Milt and I undertook together.

I first met Milt in 1989, when the advertising agency where I worked was engaged to provide advertising and promotional services for a new start-up festival, the Canadian International Dragon Boat Festival, on a pro bono basis. Since I was the only Asian at the agency, it seemed natural (and perhaps somewhat predictable) that I be given the assignment.

I invited myself to a committee meeting of the fledgling festival without knowing whether I'd be welcome. When the discussion turned to marketing, the festival's marketing manager abruptly turned the topic over to me. Nervous, I blurted out whatever was on my mind. A few days later, my blubbering words turned into the advertising plan for the festival. Talk about flying by the seat of your pants.

Over the next two years, I found myself head of the festival's marketing department—but now with my own marketing agency. As we approached the third year of the festival, something startling happened—the entire staff was fired. It seemed that, although the festival had already become an important addition to the summertime fabric of Vancouver, operations had racked up three consecutive years of losses, and something had to be done.

Soon afterwards, my phone rang. It was Milton asking for a meeting. Seeing the pink slips that had gone to my colleagues, I was sure I was next. But as we sat and discussed the festival, the unexpected happened: instead of firing me, Milt asked if I would consider running the festival as its general manager. I was flabbergasted. Why me, someone who had no experience managing a festival? As Milton gently explained, he had always been impressed with the marketing of the festival. My experience in running an advertising agency would surely give me some expertise in running an enterprise like a festival, wouldn't it? Besides, I was young. Above all, if I couldn't do the job, they'd just shut down the festival. That last piece of information was a motivating force. I didn't want to see the end of the festival or of the role it was already serving in the community.

When I asked Milt how he'd like me to proceed in my new position, he responded in a way that I've since come to know as generosity: "Make the festival the best event you can and pay down the debt." Aside from that, Milt gave me the authority to do what I wanted. Whom to hire and how to move forward truly were up to me.

With the Dragon Boat Festival, I inherited an inspiring mandate: to foster multicultural understanding. Or, put another way, to foster inclusivity among the diverse cultures of B.C. This mandate was one that Milton himself had inherited. Many years before, the late, great David Lam had provided the spark for the Dragon Boat Festival and its vision of multicultural understanding.

In the late 1980s, Vancouver experienced a demographic shift as a surge of immigrants from Hong Kong and China chose the city as their new home. In the midst of this social upheaval, the defamatory term "Hongcouver" was coined. David Lam's response to this was quintessentially David: let's create an opportunity for Vancouverites and newcomers to learn about each other, fostering an environment of cultural understanding. It was David's idea that a dragon boat festival, with its collaborative team environment, could accomplish this goal. However, then Governor General Jeanne Sauvé had just tapped David to serve as B.C.'s lieutenant-governor. He would be the first individual of Chinese descent to serve in this post. As a result, he needed someone to help realize the inaugural dragon boat festival and its mission of cross-cultural understanding. David thought there would be no one better than Milton Wong to do this, and he was right.

Over the next few years Milt, as festival chairman, and I worked together to make the festival the largest and most celebrated dragon boat event in North America. In 1996, we hosted the World Championship Dragon Boat Festival, marking the first time the global championship had been staged outside Asia. Dragon boat teams from around the world descended on Vancouver. We also inaugurated the chic and much-ballyhooed annual Dragon Boat Gala Dinner. This was at a time when chicken dinners were still, well, chicken dinners. But the festival's celebration of culture allowed a diversity of colour and expression to find its way into the dinner's theme, decor, auction, menu and, of course, illustrious guests.

With Milton, there were many firsts, and we both relished the spirit, creativity and entrepreneurship that came with doing something new and significant for the first time. And yes, along the way, we paid down the festival's debt, too. Remarkably, Milt never "managed" me or told me what to do. It was truly a collaborative relationship.

The success of the Dragon Boat Festival came back to Milton's sense of inclusivity—inclusivity of cultures and inclusivity of community—and his ability to impart the importance of that to others. During my tenure with the festival, this vision was the foundation for everything we did. Today, the Dragon Boat Festival has become a mainstay in the summertime festival scene in Vancouver, and it has inspired the creation of many other dragon boat events in B.C., Canada and the United States. I attribute its longevity and leadership to the strong vision infused by Milton, one of many important legacies he leaves us. In this case, fittingly, it's a celebration.

Sonny Wong *is an award-winning creative director and marketing entrepreneur, with a diversity of business interests and projects that span marketing/media, live programs and events, sustainability, arts and culture, creativity and social innovation. He is active in the community and participates on a number of non-profit boards.*

This piece was purchased from Sam Robinson, a Haisla artist and uncle to Lyle Wilson, whose work Milton also supported and enjoyed. Milton's relationship with the Haisla Nation began through his position as a board member of Alcan, which saw him make frequent trips to Kitimat, a small, picturesque and isolated village on B.C.'s northwest coast surrounded by coastal mountains. The Haisla had struggled with the industrialization of their community and its impact on the environment and their hunting and fishing traditions. Through close consultation with the Haisla Nation, Milton was able to garner support for a visionary plan to reduce unemployment and transform the community's future. Milton was instrumental in Alcan's landmark agreement in principle with the Haisla Nation and was a part of stimulating economic growth in the region. Later, as chancellor of SFU, Milton spearheaded training and capacity-building programs in Kitimat designed and supported by SFU.

Beaver Frontlet
SAM ROBINSON | 1995

Milton's
Paradise Found

MILTON WONG AND I worked together for more than fifteen years. Our numerous collaborations included projects with the Laurier Institution and the Wosk Centre for Dialogue, sustainability workshops and a myriad of Downtown Eastside community-based initiatives. Of the many opportunities I had to work with Milton, perhaps the most memorable was related to our work with First Nations in northern B.C.: specifically, the work we began in 2002 with the Haisla First Nation in Kitimat.

Milton, then chancellor of SFU and a philanthropist of note, had approached me to join him on a project involving the Haisla tribal council and Alcan (now Rio Tinto). I had established a relationship with Haisla chief councillor Steve Wilson through my work with the Vancouver Foundation, which had supported several projects in Haisla territory. Milton asked if I could set up a meeting with the chief to discuss their relationship with Alcan.

Milton had an uncanny ability to identify the potential in people and blend that with a deep passion and a vision for a better world. He also had a gift for taking big ideas and making them real, local and practical. He created a lot of extra work for those around him, but his passion and leadership were contagious, and he inspired people to rise to the challenge.

We headed north in a small plane in the middle of a January snowstorm. We weren't sure whether we would be able to land in Kitimat, let alone what would become of the meeting. The snow was three feet deep when we got there. It was cold outside and even colder in the room. The Alcan executives were there in force, and across the table the tribal council and elders sat quietly sizing them up. Both groups were visibly skeptical about the session.

had an uncanny ability to identify the potential in people and blend that with a deep passion and a vision for a better world.

As co-facilitators, Milton and I sat between the two factions and outlined the goals and purpose of the day. Our objective was to create a relationship protocol, a memorandum of understanding that recognized the past, addressed the issues of the present and created a blueprint of trust for the future. Alcan wanted to rebuild their fifty-year-old aluminum smelter and needed the support of the Haisla to do so. The Haisla's past experiences with local industry had not been positive; they had seen the wealth created in their territories benefit others, leaving their people with little and their lands forever changed and damaged. Our task was to create a long-term agreement that would be beneficial for both parties. It wasn't going to be easy.

And yet, eight hours later we had shaped what would become a relationship protocol, based on the following set of agreed principles: mutual understanding and openness, commitment, respect, racial harmony, patience and trust. The protocol eventually led to a transfer of land from Alcan back to the Haisla and later a multimillion-dollar transfer of funds into an educational trust for the community. Other initiatives grew out of the process, too, including the creation of the Kitimat Valley Institute, a training facility for Haisla youth. But perhaps more than anything, the protocol changed the dynamic in the area from one of dependency to one of active engagement in economic opportunities that for more than fifty years had excluded the First Nation.

Milton worked on many other projects involving First Nations. He believed that bringing people together could result in positive opportunities. Business acumen with a focus on social justice lay at the core. By working together, Milton believed, people can address past injustices in a mutually beneficial and constructive way.

Although the work is far from over, Milton's early contributions and innovative spirit helped transform a history of suspicion and skepticism into a relationship of trust and possibility. "This is a mission, not a job or project," he told me. "If we can deliver, we will change the way things are done in this province." Milton was all about change.

I will never forget those days, nor will I ever forget Milton: busy, surrounded by people seeking his guidance and leadership, yet always available for a conversation, a laugh, a moment to talk about family and friends. I am proud to say that he was a mentor, a confidant and—more than anything—a friend. I miss him.

Mauro Vescera *has worked in the non-profit field for more than twenty years and currently is employed as the executive director of the Italian Cultural Centre.*

A Man for
Many Seasons

VIVIDLY REMEMBER MY first impressions of Milton Wong. I was taken by his intellectual curiosity, his enthusiasm and the great smile that told me our exchange would far surpass my initial expectations. Over the years that followed, I remained in awe of Milton's varied interests and grateful that we shared many causes and projects.

During the 1990s, Alcan was embroiled in controversy in B.C. over its Kemano Completion Project, its Kitimat smelter and its contentious relationships with Aboriginal peoples. Milton was always willing to share his views and his contacts, and both proved seminal in forging resolutions. His advice was unconditional and his questions were incisive, leaving us with the certainty that there was a better way—and that "Uncle Milt" was pointing us in that direction. He was an example for me and for many others in Alcan.

Milt gently steered Alcan into community involvement in support of the Dragon Boat Festival and other projects. As a consequence, Alcan found itself rebranded, and with Milt's gentle encouragement and example, the company was able to resolve decades of friction with both the Haisla and the Cheslatta peoples. Milt was too good a pass for Alcan, and he was invited to sit on the Alcan Inc. board of directors. There, his eyes and all-knowing smile would signal to us that on issues such as health, safety and sustainable development, he not only supported what we were proposing but, more importantly, knew where we were going.

Our objective was to create a sustainable business model that would add value to Alcan's bottom line. Milt's innate understanding of young people and their concerns over sustainable development spoke of understanding, empathy and a profound wisdom. He pushed us to recruit young people and listen to them. Milt was an advocate for active listening and proactive comportment. He practised this continually. At first, when he stood at a meeting and moved from a comfortable chair to lean against the wall, we thought he had back problems. But we soon learned this indicated intense concentration and interest as he prepared to comment or question.

Active listening is a true art, but Milt could also hold his own with the toughest business or financial expert, always able to surprise with his questions and comments about a particular course of action. His batting average impressed me as he moved effortlessly from finance to environmental, social and community issues. He did so in a civil manner, always measured and calm regardless of the panic levels around him. I cannot remember Milt out of kilter or heated; he was a living example of quiet achievement.

Stories abound about Milt's professional endeavours, but the moments I cherished most were personal times with Milton and Fei. Sometimes we met at the Vancouver Club for a simple lunch and good conversation. Other times, Milt would carve out a visit to one of his projects, whether a renewable energy undertaking, a health innovation or a Downtown Eastside development project and social housing complex.

He was also a wonderful cook. With Fei's help, he designed and then enjoyed a kitchen meant to produce good Chinese food. My ambition is still to improve my cooking abilities so that I deserve a kitchen like that. Milt taught me how to prepare bok choy in a simple but elegant way and how to bring out the best in a dish that I still make to impress my friends and family.

It was Milt's concern for people that allowed him to move effectively in and between different worlds. Whether he was talking with business, environmental or social groups, with experts in economics or human health or development, Milt spoke from a core set of values, providing consistent, balanced and wise advice. His seemingly innocent questions contained nuggets that awakened consciousness in others. In some instances his interventions contained a time-release explosion that went to the core values of the individual or the organization. Milt promoted the idea of epiphanies. He posed his questions with a glint in his eyes and a soupçon of a smile on his lips. Those of us who were Milt watchers soon came to realize when the game was afoot.

Milt encouraged innovation and invested in ideas that made a difference. For me, he was a friend and a mentor who represented a zest for life and a fearlessness of spirit. Milton Wong was a man of and for his time. What more can one person ask of another?

Dan Gagnier is chair of the board for the International Institute for Sustainable Development. An ex-diplomat, deputy minister, chief of staff to two provincial premiers and senior executive for Alcan Inc., Dan worked with Milton Wong over several decades.

Zwischenraum (Konus)

WOLFGANG KESSLER | 2005

Inspired by German artist Wolfgang Kessler's series
of views from Germany's fast train, Fei and Milton took
the fast train during the FIFA World Cup in Germany.

Zwischenraum (Ponton)

WOLFGANG KESSLER | 2003

The Power of Big Ideas

AS A BUSINESSMAN and an entrepreneur, Milton Wong's successes were well known. He was one of the early pioneers, along with Phillips, Hager & North, in creating a significant wealth management industry in Vancouver. Milton also "rolled the dice" in many start-up ventures, from cancer treatment and early diagnostic services to green technology, such as photo voltaic solar panels.

However, I think Milton will be best remembered not for his wealth creation or his management success but for being a role model and a mentor, for showing us all how to be active, effective citizens in a democracy. From his efforts to promote corporate social responsibility to his willingness to confront difficult issues, such as immigration, race relations, multiculturalism, and a new relationship with Aboriginal communities, Milton had an amazing impact.

I was a friend and collaborator of Milton's for many years. He and I served together on the Nisga'a Lisims Government's Commercial Group of Companies board of directors. In his capacity as a director, Milton helped to develop successful business plans, financial plans and governance systems. He stressed that the Nisga'a people shouldn't get just "crumbs off the table" from the resource development involving mining, gas, hydro, tourism, forestry and fisheries in their territory in the Nass Valley and beyond. Milton relentlessly pushed for a new relationship in which the Nisga'a were majority partners; had equity positions; and could create long-term training, employment and wealth. He promoted the same model for the Haisla people in and around Kitimat.

MILTON will be best remembered not for his wealth creation or his management success but for being a role model and a mentor.

I have also been caught up in Milton and Michael Clague's long-term vision for transforming Vancouver's Downtown Eastside. Milton's holistic vision, using the Ismaili approach to community development, inspired us to form the Building Community Society. A citizen-led, city-initiated local area planning program that will result in a transformative, holistic, integrated vision for the neighbourhood.

Milt's other skill, after inspiring people with his big-idea vision, was to motivate others. I am one of many people who were lured willingly into participating in his ideas and projects. Milton's presence profoundly improved Vancouver, British Columbia, and Canada. Thank you, Milton.

Mike Harcourt *is the former mayor of Vancouver and the former premier of British Columbia.*

MILTON K. WONG

A Sustainable Downtown Eastside:
Creating Positive Change through Dialogue

SPEECH PRESENTED TO THE METRO VANCOUVER FUTURE
OF THE REGION SUSTAINABILITY SUMMIT, OCTOBER 7, 2008

'M THE KIND of guy who is always happiest when championing a good cause. I've been told my enthusiasm is infectious. And I've been talking about sustainability for at least five years now, so my passionate views on that are no secret. I suppose that explains what I'm doing standing here before you today.

In a way, I suppose I'm also the poster boy for open-minded, positive change. Just think about it: I've spent my whole career in the investment world. I built an entire company whose existence was predicated on the notion that what we are all after is growth—endless growth, limitless expansion, continuously swelling bottom lines.

And look at me now. I still lead a global bank, but I've realized that corporate growth—any growth, really—needs to be sustainable. It turns out you can't have infinite growth without eventually burning through all of the natural resources our Earth has to offer. This fact dawned on me some five or six years ago when I realized, through my work with the B.C. Cancer Foundation, that all living matter has the same DNA code—that on a cellular level, we're all the same. We're all related—you, me, an earthworm, a dolphin, a blade of grass.

Soon after that, I attended Canadian astronaut Julie Payette's convocational address to the graduating class of Simon Fraser University. She described how she saw the earth from space: how it looked beautiful but fragile, held together by the thin layer we know as the biosphere. She also said she was saddened to notice a huge plume of smoke over Indonesia because of the forest fires raging at the time. Propelled by upper air currents, the smoke was spreading around the world. It hit me again: I thought, wow, we are all in this together. As global citizens, we have a responsibility to all living things, including each other.

My conversion became final after a visit to the American Museum of Natural History in New York City. I saw a film there entitled *The Beginning of Time* about Earth's origins. A line from the movie is still etched in my brain. "Since the beginning of time," said the narrator, "matter is no more and no less than it is today."

I realized then that there is no such thing as "growth," really. Our space is limited; our Earth is finite. What we use excessively here, we deplete there. I recognized then that we also have a role to play in Third World development— a responsibility towards people on the other side of the world as well.

The point is: My intellectual and philosophical framework had been based on perpetual growth, but it was becoming apparent to me that our economic and business models did not include the notional costs of the air and water we use, not to mention the destruction of habitats required by the animal kingdom.

I don't know if words can properly convey the way these personal epiphanies turned my existing value system on its head. I've been working ever since to promote sustainability. And if a few words from a cancer society, an astronaut and a film could shift my values by 180 degrees, then there's every reason to believe that other people may also be persuaded to consider sustainability in a new way, with an open mind—for example, all of you.

Now, sustainability doesn't just refer to environmental issues. In its broadest sense, the principles of sustainability are really about ensuring that whether the subject is forests, businesses or communities, our approach to managing them doesn't sacrifice the interests of future generations.

On the weekend, I was listening to the CBC's Michael Enright discussing climate change and global warming with a panel of five people who represented different constituencies in Canada. It was evident to me that their answers were grounded in very different basic assumptions. We have yet to achieve a common understanding of sustainable living. Given that you're highly likely to encounter similarly disparate groups in Metro Vancouver, I suggest you develop a set of values or principles that will frame your policy work in sustainable living.

This is an idea that worked very well for former UN Secretary-General Kofi Annan when he developed the UN Global Compact. Annan asked all corporations worldwide to voluntarily abide by ten key principles that focus on social and environmental values as well as human rights and ethical business practices. Today, nearly four thousand major corporations have joined the compact. These companies come from all over the world, operate in dozens of different languages, have any number of different corporate cultures, come in all sizes and shapes and sell a wide variety of products or services. Yet they've all promised to be guided by the ten principles set out in the compact, because they can agree on this particular set of values.

This idea that positive change can happen when a group of very different people come together and agree on a set of values and principles grounded in sustainability can work for you, too. Like forests or oceans, communities can be managed in a sustainable way.

Sustainable communities everywhere in the world have certain things in common: Fresh air. Clean water. Public transit. Plentiful green spaces. Safe, healthy environments. Opportunities for recreation. They achieve a balance between environmental sustainability and economic growth. We must have some level of growth for adequate renewal, of course. Just not at the cost of a community's environmental integrity. Now, in that context, consider the Downtown Eastside here in Vancouver and ask yourselves: How sustainable is that community?

There are 2,500 homeless people in the Downtown Eastside now. Yet there is not one public water tap. Quite aside from what these people should do when they're thirsty, how do they even wash their feet? Within two weeks, we'll be having rain incessantly here in Vancouver, and all of these people will be out in it. And it's a problem that is constantly on the edge of becoming significantly worse: another five thousand people in the area are one cheque away from being homeless.

So ask yourselves: How did the beautiful city of Vancouver come to be responsible for what is famously known as Canada's poorest postal code—home base to thousands of people with drug problems or mental challenges?

It is my belief that misguided government policies were behind many of the wrong turns in that neighbourhood's history.

I think much of the Downtown Eastside's history has been forgotten—or at least overwritten by the dramatic drug, crime and prostitution problems that have plagued it in recent years, not to mention the controversy over the safe drug injection site, Insite. So I'd like to uncover some of that history for you today. Maybe in the context of that history, we can begin to understand what needs to happen next to return that neighbourhood to a state of normalcy and make it truly sustainable. Perhaps the next time you create a policy, you will think back to my comments today and be inspired to think more broadly and deeply, not just about what you're trying to achieve but about your policy's potential unintended effects.

It's a little-known fact that the decline of the Downtown Eastside can be traced to the internment of nearly 22,000 Japanese Canadians in 1942. The vast majority of them were Canadians living in British Columbia, and the Downtown Eastside was home to many of them. Thanks to government policy, all Japanese residents of that neighbourhood were removed within one week. Their internment devastated what was then one of Vancouver's most vibrant communities, launching it into seventy years of progressive degeneration.

By the early 1950s, the City of Vancouver had declared large parts of the Downtown Eastside a slum. The city's plan for addressing the problem included an urban renewal policy that rescinded basic city services, denied building permits and prevented families in the area from renovating their homes to accommodate their growing needs. I'm well aware of this myself, because my family was among them—we tried three times to apply for such a permit. In the end, many families, including mine, were forced to move to other neighbourhoods.

That's a strange recipe for urban renewal, if you ask me, and its results were predictable: the area lost its heart and soul and began instead to resemble an empty shell. Next, the city shut down the Greater Vancouver interurban rail system in favour of buses and cars. Running all the way downtown from Chilliwack, the system had once made the Downtown Eastside a central hub. Closing it isolated the area even further.

An empty shell is easily collapsed, and the neighbourhood's descent into chaos and despair was hastened by additional short-sighted policies enacted over the next few decades by more senior levels of government, such as the closure of mental health facilities like the 5,500-bed Riverview psychiatric facility in Coquitlam. When most of the hospital was closed down without appropriate alternatives or supports offered in its place, its former inhabitants (and many others in need of such services) migrated to the Downtown Eastside. Essentially, 5,500 mentally ill people were relocated from a hospital to the streets of the Downtown Eastside—without beds, without meds, without adequate front-line doctors, nurses or supports of any kind.

The federal government's decision to cut back on social housing in the early 1990s—production came to a halt in 1993—ensured that the neighbourhood would sink into a nearly irreversible state of decline. In 1993, the flagship Woodward's store on Abbott—which had been just a block away from the interurban rail system—closed. Numerous other businesses and restaurants followed suit, completing the area's destruction.

WITH HINDSIGHT, IT'S obvious that a series of ill-advised government policies drove people into a community that lacked both the capacity and the infrastructure to respond practically or politically. Having stripped the community of leadership and torn out its soul, the city then began to stuff the void with people who weren't welcome anywhere else. That unfortunate tradition continues today. There seems to be an unwritten policy to drive prostitution towards the Downtown Eastside, away from Mount Pleasant and the West End.

Inevitably, the Downtown Eastside has become a dubious sanctuary for those with few choices. Although historically the area has always welcomed misfits, a criminal element eventually emerged. With cuts to income assistance, crimes of desperation have increasingly plagued its streets.

Millions—if not tens of millions—of dollars have been spent trying to fix the Downtown Eastside. Where are the results? Unravelling and remedying the seven decades' worth of misguided government policies that have led to the area's many problems is proving to be a tougher proposition than anyone imagined.

When it comes to providing social housing for people with low or no income, government funding is certainly critical—and appreciated. But history would seem to indicate that government involvement in the many other complexities attached to intractable social problems is often counterproductive.

What the area needs is not more government policies, interventions or handouts. Instead, the approach I'm recommending—indeed, the one I'm taking—is one I've learned through my work with the Aga Khan Foundation Canada: that any kind of assistance must be based on dialogue with the community and its leaders.

Simply put, we must begin to talk to the people who live there. We have to learn from the community we're trying to help, just as they are learning from us. There needs to be a mutual exchange of information. The idea is that education works both ways; the focus is on empowering people to help themselves. Consistently, dialogue with the community on health, housing, economic self-sufficiency and cultural development has been the key to success.

These are the elements that will cause the Downtown Eastside to become self-sustaining. Through my volunteer work with the Carnegie Community Centre, I've discovered that the area does still have a heartbeat. It has people who still feel passion for community life. More than one hundred of them showed up at the one-hundredth anniversary of Carnegie in 2003 and volunteered to be part of the Heart of the City Festival. They later mounted a one-act opera on drug addiction. To me, this is evidence that the people living there are passionate about their community and its soul. And I think we can all learn from that.

To conclude, I would say that the Downtown Eastside is the most challenging social issue we are facing in Vancouver. There is no time for wringing of hands. We have a chance right now to right a series of wrongs through dialogue. And with the Winter Olympics scheduled to take place here in 2010, we may find ourselves at a turning point. The provincial government may be on the receiving end of increasing international pressure to address the problems of the Downtown Eastside. How will it go about doing that?

It was interesting to notice how a small tent city that sprouted in Oppenheimer Park this summer was hastily dismantled by police while Premier Gordon Campbell was in Beijing, attending the Olympics and being interviewed about Vancouver's homeless problem. One likes to think this had more to do with concern for people's personal safety than with concern for appearances. And it is nice that the tent-dwellers were offered rooms in nearby residential hotels. But how do you explain how they ended up with housing overnight, essentially jumping the queue ahead of people who had been waiting for months?

We need a solution for the Downtown Eastside that is permanent, not cosmetic and short term. We need to be motivated by compassion, not politics. We need to address the problem head-on by talking to the people who live there, not by handing them one-way bus tickets out of town. Many of you are policy-makers. I hope that rather than simply rubbing you the wrong way today with my talk of foolhardy government policies, I've inspired you to return to work feeling passionate about creating better ones.

Perhaps our new policy for sustainable development in the Downtown Eastside could be as simple as this: We will talk to the people who live there to see what they need. And then we will help them learn to meet those needs themselves so that they will be driven by a sense of purpose and rewarded by a sense of accomplishment. We need to give them a hand up, not just a handout.

Do I have a seconder?

Thank you.

THREE

It's Not Just about the Money

From a series described as "calligraphy with cigarette burns"
by contemporary Shanghai artist Wang Tiande.
Produced and initially exhibited at Centre A in Vancouver.

Chinese Clothes No. 05-D02
WANG TIANDE | 2005

Where the
Puck Ends Up

I F YOU RELATED Milton Wong's leadership ability to the athletic world, it's like he saw things other athletes couldn't see. What made Wayne Gretzky a great athlete was his vision: to go where the puck was going to end up. Milton's abilities were like that.

I started off as Milton's stockbroker. I was passionate about finance, and I had taken an aptitude test. I loved the markets, so I became a stockbroker. I didn't really like being a stockbroker, though, because back then there was a huge conflict of interest. You got paid on commission, so you weren't really a money manager; you were a salesperson. I wanted to get in on the business side.

When Milt started his own firm in 1981, I thought I would really like to work at M.K. Wong and Associates. Why not work at the best place in town? Milt had a superman reputation. My late grandfather, who was on the advisory board of National Trust, was a big fan of Milt. I idolized my grandfather, so even before I had met Milt, I thought the world of him. Once he founded M.K. Wong, I'd phone him up and take him out for lunch and tell him: "You should hire me!" Initially, M.K. Wong only managed pension fund business and didn't have a private arm. But when Peter Malcolm got there, he established a private arm at the company. Eventually, Peter got in touch, and I was hired at M.K. Wong in 1986.

Milt hired great people who produced great results. M.K. Wong was a great firm, because Milt had a knack for choosing talented people. One young guy came down to Vancouver looking for a job and somehow got an interview with Milt. Milt hired him, even though the company wasn't looking for anybody. There was no job opening. This breaks all the rules of HR. But as a consequence, Milt ended up with interesting people who otherwise wouldn't have been hired.

Milt was brilliant about challenging people intellectually. People liked that. It surprised them, too, since most financial institutions are very boring. Milt would talk about something totally outside of the box and get away with it. I remember he put on a three-day seminar for our clients. Nobody else would do that. It was really expensive. He brought in speakers from all over, and I know the clients loved it.

Milt was human and not perfect. Although his vision and his ability to see into the future were unbelievable, his day-to-day skills were not. I remember once he took me to see some small software company where he held a personal position. He was spending all day at this tiny company, when M.K. Wong managed $3.5 billion.

I had such nerve. We were driving across the Burrard Street Bridge, and I said "Milt, we can't even buy the stock from that company. It's so small, it wouldn't have an impact on any portfolio. Shouldn't we be spending the day trying to decide whether it's Commerce Bank or Bank of Nova Scotia we should be having in our portfolios?"

And he said, with great distaste, "That's boring."

Milt was a very perceptive guy and a very good listener. We went out for lunch once with a senior tax advisor. I was impressed by this person, and Milt was always generous with his time. Whenever I told him, "You really have to meet this person," he was helpful. That day, as we were walking back to the office after lunch, Milt said to me, "That guy is a piranha." I said, "What? That guy is amazing!" In the end, Milt was right. The guy was a piranha. But it took me a decade to realize it.

Milt was also a model for being informed. I remember one time, we're talking '86 or '87, he was stoked about fibre optics. We were like, "What's fibre optics?" And he was right, of course. It was revolutionary.

I think the real legacy of M.K. Wong is all the other firms it spawned. If he had simply gone to work for another top firm, it would have been a disaster for the city. There wouldn't have been the critical mass of firms we have now to hire young people and keep them here, to train people, to manage money. Milt was cool in that he started from scratch and built a real firm. He spawned my firm and all these other firms. We've created a forest. We manage way more than the wealth of British Columbia in Vancouver's money management firms, too. M.K. Wong and Associates was one of the reasons this is possible.

There are so few women in the investment world. It's because we are not risk-takers. What girls need more than anything is to fail. Fail, fail, fail, then get up and do it again. Women hate failure, so we don't take risks. We don't invest big bucks, we don't put our life on the line, put our career on the line, put our opportunity on the line. Milt had three daughters and was sensitive to the challenges that professional women face. He was very encouraging and open to helping women achieve success.

What gets me up in the morning and makes me drive across town and fight the traffic are my clients. I have an amazing passion to serve wealthy people who don't understand the markets. You just feel so good when you help somebody. If I can put the puck in the net, make the light go on and help somebody make their money last for the rest of their lives, that's very, very enjoyable. Milton Wong was committed to his passions. He worked hard to be successful and inspired many (including me) to be the best we can be.

Leslie Cliff, *born in Vancouver in 1955, swam on Canada's national team for six years, which included winning a silver medal in the 1972 Olympics. She co-founded Genus Capital Management in 1989 and continues as chairman of Genus today. She has received the Order of Canada, is an honorary chartered accountant and serves on the board of Swimming Canada.*

Stewards
of Capital

ATTENDED UBC, STUDYING finance in their business school. When I was close to graduation, the dean asked me what I'd like to do. I said I'd like to be involved in the money management industry, and he said, "Well, you should definitely go talk to Milton Wong." So I came down and talked to Milton and to Bob DeHart, who was head of fixed income at M.K. Wong and Associates at that time. Probably Milton's most aggressive question was "Are you absolutely sure you want to do fixed income?"

Historically, fixed income was viewed as a wayward stop on the path to managing equities. M.K. Wong wanted someone to focus on bonds to make sure that was the case. I joined in May of '93, and I remember my starting salary was more than I thought I would ever make in the industry. It was more than my parents made, and I was amazed at it. It was such a learning experience to work with Milton and Bob. Their willingness to transfer their knowledge of financial markets and managing money really gave someone starting in the industry the benefit of their lifetimes of experience.

One of the challenges in investment markets is that things never repeat, but they frequently rhyme. When you're starting out in the industry, everything seems so new. Both Milton and Bob were incredibly giving in terms of their time, in talking through the crises that had occurred in the '70s and the '80s, how they built up their firm and the investment decisions they made. I use some of their experiences and knowledge base to this day when managing money.

I think what was unique about working with Milton was how excited he would get about certain ideas or opportunities. I frequently found when we worked together that he would have a vision of "Well, we could do this," and then it would be up to me to figure out, "Okay, what are the steps we would have to take to get to that?"

One of our big pushes in the '90s while I was there was building out expertise and investment strategies for foundations and endowments. Milton strongly believed that foundations and endowments in general were under-served in terms of their money management capabilities. Part of a money manager's responsibility is education. You need to look at it not as solely managing a client's money and making decisions. Part of your role is to make sure they understand why you are making those decisions on their behalf so that they can become better stewards of their capital.

Milton talked a lot about how money managers are guardians of capital, whereas investment banks are merchants of capital. He believed strongly in that idea. Part of the education process was a handbook we developed for foundations and endowments. Milton took that project from a germination of "Wouldn't this be interesting," and in the end I think it was a couple of hundred pages long. It was very well received.

The thing that was unique about Milton was his ability to see two or three steps further than what other people could visualize. It was having a faith or a willingness or a vision—I don't know how you want to term it—but just this confidence that something that seemed insurmountable could happen. Whether it was setting up the portfolio management program at UBC or my example of the foundation and endowment side or just demon-strating what a money management business could look like, Milton was able to develop his vision and articulate it in a way that got people excited about moving towards that vision. To go with him was one of the most exciting paths you'd ever be on.

In my view, it was almost like a gut sense with him. He would see a lot of different ideas, but maybe one in ten of those ideas captured his imagina-tion. I don't think it was necessarily him sitting in a dark room coming up

THE thing that was unique about Milton was his ability to see two or three steps further than what other people could visualize.

with different things. He was very gregarious; he was out there talking to different people, getting these different ideas. One in ten would spark something in him, and then he'd start thinking about it and come up with various aspects, and he'd talk about it with other people and get their views. And then suddenly, over the course of a few months, he was able to blossom that one little germination idea, that one little conversation, into something much larger. It wasn't strategic vision, in the traditional sense of sitting down in a dark room and figuring it out. It was much more social, in terms of how he took those ideas and got them to the point where you could actually articulate them.

First and foremost, M.K. Wong and Associates was a partnership, and that engendered this collegial atmosphere in terms of people working together. It was really exciting being in that type of smaller firm. Milton was always the head of the firm, in terms of both shareholding and day-to-day decision making, but he also delegated a lot of decisions, whether on the operation side or in fixed income and equities, and he was very comfortable, once he'd built up that trust, in terms of delegation.

It was an incredibly exciting place to work, because of Milton's willingness to accept new ideas and look at new approaches. Very infrequently it was "We can't do that" or "That can't be done, because we haven't done it before." A lot of the constructs that get in the way of an organization's ability to evolve weren't there at M.K. Wong.

Later on, when Milton looked at the global investment marketplace and the changing needs of Canadian investors, he saw increasingly that plans would have to look at a larger proportion of their assets getting managed outside of Canada. When I first joined, the pension plan rule was that no more than 10 per cent could get invested in foreign equities. That was bumped up to 20, and then 30, and so on. I think Milton saw those trends as meaning that it wasn't possible to be a purely domestic money manager any longer. I think a part of him was disappointed at losing some of those cultural aspects of partnership and some of the innovations that a smaller firm can deliver, but he also realized that for us to fulfill our stewardship of capital, we needed to have capabilities beyond what we could deliver ourselves. By joining with HSBC, one of the world's largest financial institutions, we were able to deliver resources that we couldn't as an independent firm.

We sold M.K. Wong to HSBC in May of '96, and I stayed with the firm until March 2001. I was on the board of directors for a time, and Milton was chairman of the board. For my final two years, I worked with him on board responsibilities. He would always give solid advice—he was an effective chairman by any measure—but I don't think he ever got the same level of enjoyment out of the company after we sold. For the first couple of years, there's a lot of transition, and so that was an exciting time period, but post-transition I think it was a little more frustrating for him.

Milt always had his Chinese heritage as a source of pride. But I remember a few funny episodes. Sometimes we would take prospective investors or clients out for a Chinese dinner or dim sum lunch, and Milton would try to show off his Cantonese, which we all know was never the best. He would try to order something, and then invariably the server would say, "Oh, you want a napkin" back to him in English. No matter what he tried, it just never quite worked out. I also remember him being convinced that because of the Bering Strait land bridge theory, the Chinese and the First Nations were interlinked, and that would give us an edge on winning First Nations bids. He was going to use that in his pitches.

Probably the biggest personal impact on me was the time I spent with Milton outside of work. There were two things. One was his insistence on baking pies for charity. So, every winter, he and I would bake huge sets of pies. I still use the same pie crust recipe to this day. I have so many fond memories of Milton's huge thumbs. He was always convinced that we could sell these pies for a couple of hundred dollars each, because he'd helped make them and the money was going to charity. The other thing was the value he put on making time for family. I have a young daughter and son now, and Milton's example has been a huge impact in terms of realizing that your work can provide a lot of enjoyment, but at the end of the day, your family has to be of primary importance. He demonstrated that.

My wife and I spent eight or nine years in the San Francisco Bay Area, California, coming back once a year to visit family and friends. A lot changed during that time. Now that I'm back in Vancouver, I have even more respect for the mark Milton made on the city. It's only by getting some perspective that you can really see what a unique person he was and what a unique influence he had. Seeing it all with fresh eyes, I value both his contribution and the time that he spent with me even more than I did before.

Jim Gilliland *is currently the head of fixed income for Leith Wheeler Investment Counsel, an independently owned investment counsel based in Vancouver. After working with Milton Wong at M.K. Wong and Associates and HSBC Global Asset Management, Jim earned his master's degree in financial engineering at the University of California, Berkeley.*

Milton making
his famous apple pie.

MILTON WONG'S
Famous Apple Pie

PASTRY	FILLING
2 cups flour	10 local organic B.C. apples, sliced thin
½ tsp salt	
⅓ cup lard	1½ tsp cinnamon
⅓ cup butter	½ cup sugar
5–9 Tbsp water	

MILTON'S APPLE PIES were so good he was known to raffle them off for charity. He first got the recipe from his wife Fei's granduncle, and it was so delicious he learned how to make it himself.

TO MAKE the pastry, sift the flour and salt together. Cut the lard/butter mix into pea-size lumps. Add 3 Tbsp of water at a time, while slowly stirring in the sifted flour and salt. Repeat to a total of 9 Tbsp water, or until flour settles into big lumps.

Cupping your hands, divide the dough into two round balls. Roll out the pastry for the bottom of the pie, making sure it is solidly packed in the pan. Mix the filling and pour it into the pie shell. Add slices of butter on top of the filling. Roll out the second ball to make the "lid" of the pie. Moisten the edges of the pie shell with a little water, and then place the top crust over the apples. Tuck any excess pastry under the bottom crust, and then crimp the edges using your fingers or a fork. Using a sharp knife, make five 5-cm slits from the centre of the pie out towards the edge to allow the steam to escape.

Cover the pie with plastic wrap and place it in the refrigerator to chill the pastry while you preheat the oven. Bake for 20 minutes at 400°F, then for 25 minutes at 350°F. Sell to the highest bidder.

Opportunity
Unearthed

MILTON WONG WAS the kind of person who creates. He created a dream; he created opportunities for the generations. There are few people like that. Over the last twenty-five years, that's what Milton and I shared. When we met, I was young and passionate. I was full of energy. Milton recognized that, and that's why he treated me as an entrepreneur, as a creator and as an artist.

When I came to Canada in 1985, I had never worked in a typical job. I came here with $30. I was born in China in the 1960s, and then the Cultural Revolution hit, so I couldn't go to school. In my generation, there was no education. I pursued my education here in Canada. When I arrived, I couldn't speak or read English. But give me enough time, and I will make something happen. I am not the smartest person, but I'm not the dumbest person. So I have a fifty-fifty chance.

Milton could not speak Chinese, but he was a very traditional, solid, Chinese-heritage–minded kind of person. He transferred that to me. He said, "Don't forget you are Chinese." At that time, anyone who left China had negative emotions about their country. It was very difficult to face the reality of being Chinese. People tried to avoid it by saying they were Japanese or Korean. Milton gave me the model to feel proud to be Chinese.

Milton and I worked together over the years on investment projects and start-up businesses. Out of nowhere one day in 2005, I received a phone call from an acquaintance, who said, "Daoping, we have a problem. There's a dinosaur exhibition in Montreal trying to come to Vancouver, but we can't close a deal. Can you help us?"

Milton's support as founding partner, investor and mentor, I wouldn't be half of who I am today.

We quickly made a deal, and with my background as an artist, I also thought these fossils could be boring on their own and too traditional. I thought, let's do something different. Why don't we build some life-size animatronic dinosaur models? People said I was crazy. So I went to China for two months with my own money and built two: one T. Rex and one triceratops. We had a great dinosaur exhibition, but unfortunately, the venue where it was held went bankrupt.

During that exhibition, however, I got a call from the Toronto Zoo. The marketing director said, "We saw your exhibition and want to do a dinosaur exhibition at our zoo." I had no idea what the industry charged for something like this. Milton asked a colleague on my behalf, who said, "You're crazy. You have no experience. There's no way you're going to get a contract." But I had the vision, the passion and the commitment, so I wanted to try it. It turned out the Toronto Zoo really wanted to work with us, but my vision was more than what they had in mind. I wanted people to walk with the dinosaurs; I wanted a movie, a laser show, the whole thing. The zoo said, "Okay, we want to work with you, but here's the most we can consider for a budget, which is significantly more than we usually spend. You deliver, then we pay you. You don't deliver, then no deal." One hundred per cent of the risk was on me.

To produce these dinosaurs costs a lot of money. If you fail, everything goes down the drain—half a million dollars. I was working for Milton at the time. Because he and I had worked together for more than twenty years by this point, he trusted me. I had to raise my own money. I put up my house. I did everything I could to put that first show together. I told Milton, "The only thing I need from you is my normal paycheque. If I fail, let me go; if I win, I will pay you back." Milton agreed. May 1, 2007, was the grand opening of *Dinosaurs Alive!* at the Toronto Zoo, with twenty-two animatronic dinosaurs, four skeletons and up to twenty-five fossils. Milton was the keynote speaker. Even a week before opening, the Toronto Zoo could not advertise the exhibition, because they didn't know if I could deliver or not. But I had confidence and Milton's support.

The opening was fantastic, and it launched my company, Dinosaurs Unearthed. We're now the number-one travelling dinosaur exhibition company in the world. To date, we have had exhibitions in China, Europe and Australia and throughout Canada and the United States. We have more than four hundred dinosaurs and a complete educational package. Our style is very entertaining and educational. Without Milton's support as founding partner, investor and mentor, I wouldn't be half of who I am today.

Building a company from an idea to an industry leader requires lots of management skills. At the end of the day, it's about the people. I took so much advice from Milton on choosing people. How do you choose skilled people? How can you see if a person has potential? He was always saying that if you do everything yourself, you will never go anywhere. It doesn't matter how smart you are. You have limited time, limited capital, limited energy. How can you deliver everything? You need your people. Uncle Milt was really, really good with people. He spent 99.99 per cent of his time thinking about others. He could talk to someone for thirty minutes and come back with topics 1, 2, 3, 4 for that person. Over the years, I came to see that everything he said was correct.

What was special about Milton was that he never looked at what was happening today or had happened yesterday. He was always working with a vision and a goal to reach. In the end, Milton was always a winner. That's what made his life so interesting. He would always say, "Oh, I'm going to retire. I'm going to retire." And I would say, "You know, Uncle Milt, maybe

your body thinks you'd like to retire but not your brain. You'll never retire."
What I learned from Milton was the importance of having a vision, a goal
and the commitment to deliver—the guts to finish and never give up—
giving other people opportunities along the way, too.

Anyone can have an opportunity. It depends on your reaction when facing
that opportunity. We are all born the same. We start from nothing. We don't
know how to speak or walk. At the end of the day, you have to go back to the
earth. Life is a circle. How can you leave something for the next generation?
Like Milton, I want to create something for the future generations. How can
I help the economy? How can I help society? How can I help the environment? You have to take a risk. If you want people to trust you, you have to
trust yourself first. That's leadership, and Milton Wong was my model.

Daoping Bao *is president and* CEO *of Dinosaurs Unearthed in Richmond, B.C. He worked
with Milton Wong on this and many other projects and businesses over twenty-five years.
Milton was a partner, investor, friend and mentor whose support has made Daoping who
he is today.*

Most of Vancouver's respectable Chinese families felt
obliged, even coerced, to send their children to one of the
half dozen private Chinese schools. All parents feared their
children might become "mono," Gold Mountain (Canadian)
children who were careless of Chinese traditions. Milton
and his brothers and sisters all attended the Mon Keong
school, depicted in this photograph, every weekday and
Saturday. This image, taken by celebrated Vancouver
photographer Fred Herzog, was a gift from Alcan following
Milton's retirement from the board.

Chinese New Year 1964
FRED HERZOG | 1964

The Business of
Social Philanthropy

SIMON SUTCLIFFE: I met Milton Wong in the late '90s when I invited him to be part of a team to search for a chair in breast cancer research at the B.C. Cancer Agency. Funding for research was getting tighter, and the health care system's interest in research was on the wane. Everyone was trying to address how to stimulate innovative research, how to support it, fund it and grow it without reliance on financial support from the health care system.

Milton was one of a group of people who started to think with the B.C. Cancer Agency about how we could capture research and grow it as a business but do so in a way that some of the products of that research, including profits, could be ploughed back into cancer research and research organizations. In this way, the research environment could be nurtured and grown without reliance on government funds and without fiscal constraints on the innovation and creativity of cancer research that would have an impact.

The first incarnation of this business research enterprise was called Genyous. Initially, we were primarily interested in work that had been done in the area of medical biophysics and cancer imaging. As Genyous evolved, it separated from the company run today by Bojana Turic, Perceptronix Medical Inc., or PMI.

It was really interesting to discover a group of people like Milton, who had a vision and were pursuing it not for the money but to do something good. The idea was to save the world by helping other people through business acumen directed to social philanthropy. How do you apply that attitude to medical research? Milton was one of the few entrepreneurial people who wanted to understand that particular territory.

I suppose the characteristic that describes social entrepreneurs, and social philanthropists in general, is that they don't have to make money for themselves. They've made money and they can now afford to think about "goodness" and other things that drive human health and well-being. What I think really characterized the group of individuals who started Genyous, and led later to PMI, is that they'd moved away from personal glory, achievement and wealth to focus on what "goodness" is all about.

BOJANA TURIC: We're trying to raise awareness that if the government is not involved in supporting research, eventually the research will die and nobody will use it. In the life science community we understand that if people with good hearts are donating to research, it is because they want the research to grow and eventually be used in clinical practice. You want something that every single physician and every patient has access to. If you don't have a mechanism to make that happen, eventually the research will disappear. Or you can take the research and the product outside of Canada, which is what PMI is doing right now.

Milton invested ten years of his life and his money into PMI. Today, there are people benefitting from our work. But are we successful in Canada from the revenue point of view? No. Can we sustain ourselves just by doing sales in Canada? No. Is this system endorsing us? No. So it's a tough fight.

Ultimately, at a certain point, a private company needs to become independent of investors, and then it is all about budgets. When we were struggling with fundraising to get the company going, Milton was pushing us, saying there must be a way to generate sales in Canada: "You have to find a way. You have to think beyond boundaries." We would have these brainstorming sessions with him, turning every stone, and then finally we did find our niche. I think it was because he pushed us that we had a breakthrough. Today, there are about 650 dentists using tests based on our technology, and that number is increasing every day in Canada. We have installed our platform in many laboratories in the Asia-Pacific region, and the company is on the rise.

Milton could have gone public with PMI, but he didn't want to. He wanted to build the company to do good, to do what is right, to translate the research from the B.C. Cancer Agency and make it available to everybody. That was his drive and his passion.

SIMON SUTCLIFFE: There are two aspects to this: the vision and the drive to succeed. For Milton, failure was not an option.

BOJANA TURIC: I reminded Milton one Christmas that Winston Churchill defined success as the ability to experience failure after failure without losing enthusiasm for your goal.

SIMON SUTCLIFFE: A great quote from Albert Einstein was that he didn't know if he was brighter than anybody else; he just stayed with the problem longer. That sounds like Milton!

How you change the practice of medicine is the key piece. It's not just doing innovative things; it's causing a better outcome for people. If you don't deal with the challenges, the system can never get better. So, hard as those challenges are, frustrating and agonizing as they may be, you have to keep chipping away at them.

BOJANA TURIC: I had huge admiration for Milton and his passion for improving the quality of health care. Or was it stubbornness?

Can Milton be replicated? No, he was a unique person. I think you are born like that, and then your life shapes you as you go along. He was a good coach. He coached me and a few others at PMI. He used to say: "Never take no for an answer." We would discuss obstacles, possibilities, various pathways until we came up with a plan. And then he would say: "Hey, if this plan doesn't work, we will regroup and make another one."

Dr. Bojana Turic *is director, president and* CEO *of Perceptronix Medical Inc., a private laboratory and medical device company specializing in innovative early cancer detection tests.*

Dr. Simon Sutcliffe *is involved in national and international cancer control activities. He was formerly the president and* CEO *of the B.C. Cancer Agency and board chair of the Canadian Partnership Against Cancer.*

Because of how hard it was to get Milton to sit down for the painting, this portrait apparently took a long time to finish. Don Steele took art classes in the evenings and began painting with portraits. He would hold small art shows to raise money to support children's art programs.

Quitting
Is Not an Option

MY STORY ABOUT Milton does not involve monumental moments or great breakthroughs. It is about what comes beforehand. It is about the little things that get us there. It is about the relentless effort and undeniable faith that, like water wearing down stone, eventually prevail.

Milton changed my life in more ways than one. Some of his influences were subtle, and they took a long time to become part of my thinking and decision-making process. Others were more direct. Several years ago, for example, I was working extremely hard, logging in long hours and eating a lot of junk food along the way. One day Milton showed up at my office unannounced to tell me that I did not look good and really had to start looking after my health. That was it: a two-minute conversation. He left right afterwards, but what he said, and more importantly the way he said it, had a profound effect on my lifestyle. I still work just as hard, if not harder, but I dropped sixty pounds in slightly more than a year, and I fully intend to keep it that way.

Milton Wong was my mentor. He was my friend. My story is about two gifts that Milton gave me over the years of us working together. Two gifts that I will have with me throughout my life and hopefully one day will have an opportunity to pass along to others who dare to take on an impossible challenge. Not for the money, but for what they believe in.

Milton and I met at the time I was involved in starting up Day4 Energy, the company to which I have given much of the last eleven years. Day4 was not much more than an idea then, an idea that most people would quickly have labelled as an impossible one to realize. In fairness, the technology was neither fully developed nor patented then. It resided only in the heads of its Russian inventors. From an investment standpoint, the idea was a very tough sell. It was like a classic matryoshka doll: every time you pulled away a layer of risk, there was another one behind it.

But at the same time, there was a vision attached. A vision of a technology that could change the way we generate energy, that could make energy not only available but also affordable and accessible in places and for people who could never get it otherwise. It was a vision of doing something that could change the world. Most people would consider that too risky. Milton considered it worth doing.

We were a small group who shared that vision and the passion to realize it. Competition was stiff, the market was volatile and cash was tight. I could not count the times people told us that it could never be done. They told us that the technology could never work. They told us that we could never raise enough money. They even told us that solar energy would never power anything bigger than a calculator. But the technology did work, we did raise the money and our technology is on its way to becoming the standard in an industry that has grown a hundredfold in the last eleven years. All of this took a lot of work, but none of it would have been possible if we hadn't dared to try. And that was the first gift that Milton gave me—the confidence to believe. He taught me to listen to skeptics (after all, sometimes they are right) but never to let them bring you down. He taught me how to harness the power of one's passion to do the impossible. Milton always believed that if there was a will, there was a way.

Having the courage to start the quest is half the battle. Finishing it is a whole different story. The second gift Milton gave me was the knowledge of what it takes to finish the work you started.

Even before I met Milton, I had heard stories about him sticking it out with a business through thick and thin, even after everyone else had abandoned ship, only to see the business finally succeed. People said this was because of the incredible luck Milton had with investing. I know now that it had nothing to do with luck. On the contrary, it had everything to do with battling through challenges no matter what. For me, no matter how tough it got, Milton was always there. Whether we were battling through the financial crisis of 2008, pioneering the outsourced manufacturing model in the solar industry in 2009 or launching the solar energy manufacturing franchise in 2010, Milton gave me the strength and the inspiration to stay the course. I learned that it was not about the money. It was about doing the right thing. It was about seeing the dream come true.

Some time ago, Milton gave me a copy of a poem that I now have framed on the wall of my office. I can't recite the entire piece by heart, but there is one part that has stuck with me and will probably do so forever: "Rest if you must, but do not quit." This short passage has come to me during some of my most difficult times, and each time I was able to pick myself up.

I am not an overly emotional person, but for some reason those words overwhelm me whenever I recite them. Perhaps it is the memory of Milton reading me the line for the very first time. Or perhaps it is because that is what he did and kept doing, always, no matter how tough or desperate things got. For those who dare to try, quitting is not an option.

George Rubin *is a physicist, investment banker and entrepreneur. He is co-founder of Pacific Surf Partners Corp., an early-stage private equity investment group, as well as such technology companies as Day4 Energy, Fresco & Freddo and Clear Metals.*

The Love Bandit

KNEW MILTON WONG from the time I was a kid. My uncle Bob was his business partner at M.K. Wong. When I was in college, I'd see Milton a couple of times over the summer. And then, when I started working, we'd have dinners. At every encounter, Milton was there to share his insightful thoughts with me.

I grew up in British Columbia, but I only moved back to Vancouver eleven years ago. When I got here, the first person I called to have breakfast was Milt. I told him, "Milt, I want to start a family here. I want to settle down. And I want to start and grow a business in health care." As it turns out, Ken Sim had called Milton three days earlier, saying the same thing. Milton said to me: "Well, why don't you meet this young guy? He's really smart, and he's just moved out here as well."

Ken and I met the following week and hit it off. We started talking about different business plans for what eventually became Nurse Next Door. We went back to Milt to run our ideas by him. We wanted to start a company that took care of seniors in their homes, but we weren't doing anything new. We thought, well, maybe this isn't the right kind of business, because it's not innovative. We figured if anybody in the country could tell us "You guys are on the wrong path" or "You're absolutely on the right path," it was Milton. He had the knowledge and wisdom to really understand what would influence our society over the next twenty-five years and what our country would need.

So we went to Milt, and we said, "Here's what we want to do." I thought he might laugh at us, because we were presenting such a simple concept. I had been in high-tech before that, and Ken had been in investment banking. We didn't know how he'd respond. But as soon as we started to tell him what we wanted to do, that we felt taking care of seniors in their homes was such an important part of society, he said, "Guys, stop." He literally put his thumb up. And then he said, "Guys, I'm in. We've got to do this." He signed on to be chairman that day. We hadn't even started the company yet, and he became our chairman.

So Ken, Milton and I started Nurse Next Door together. Milton's business card actually read "Chairman and Raving Fan." He became our most passionate admirer and partner in building the business. He mentored us and helped us grow what is today the largest national brand in our vertical. We take a lot of pride in being thought leaders in senior home care in this country.

Milton could be pretty far out there, because he was a leading-edge thinker. Some of his ideas could be funny and crazy. And you might have thought, you know, that's just Milt talking again, saying some wild thing. But he had the ability to think not just a few years ahead but a *generation* ahead. He thought about how to shape our country, our society, not just our company or our personal lives. That enabled us to really stay ahead of the curve.

Milt was an incredibly curious person, and he used his curiosity better than anyone I've ever seen. He loved listening to and learning from people of all ages. He pulled information from everyone and was inspired by that.

There's a poem on the front page of our brand guide that describes Nurse Next Door. Looking at it, it dawned on me that Milton had inspired our whole concept. If you replace "she" with "he," it goes like this:

He wears a smile like a favourite T-shirt.
Like any great friend, he does what he says he's going to do.
He's action, not talk. He's light on his toes.

And he has a heart big enough to keep up a country's pulse.
Infusing calm and order into the situation is like breathing to him.
He likes clear conversations.
He's a Love Bandit,
And cooks gourmet meals in his downtimes,
And dispenses them at random, just because.

Milt was our brand. He was Nurse Next Door.

John DeHart *is the CEO of Nurse Next Door, a private home care franchise system he co-founded with business partner Ken Sim and the unwavering support of his mentor, Milton Wong. Milton, an initial investor in Nurse Next Door, served as chairman from start-up until his passing.*

Knowing Milton's work with Aboriginal communities and his deep appreciation for Aboriginal culture, Dick and Gretchen Evans, Alcan's executive director and his partner, gifted Milton with this drum.

MILTON K. WONG
Towards Sustainability: Rewriting the Script

SPEECH PRESENTED TO THE WORLD ENVIRONMENT
CENTER AND INTERNATIONAL ENVIRONMENT FORUM,
MONTREAL, QUEBEC, OCTOBER 15, 2004

THE CORPORATION AS psychopath: it was an eye-opening, attention-grabbing metaphor drawn by the minds behind the film with the same name.

Since not all of you have seen the movie *The Corporation,* I'd better tell you how its creators came up with this clever comparison. The moviemakers used the actual diagnostic criteria set out by the World Health Organization and the DSM-IV, the standard diagnostic tool used by psychiatrists, to assess the mental health of today's corporations:

· Self-interest, inherent immorality, callousness and a tendency toward deceit: Check.
· An inclination to breach social and legal standards to get what they want: Check.
· Absolute freedom from guilt, combined with the eerie ability to imitate positive human qualities such as kindness and altruism: Check.

Official diagnosis: Corporations, those organizational incarnations of who-cares capitalism, are raving psychopaths. The movie takes it further, too, accusing corporate America of harming workers and being injurious to human health, animals and the environment. Worse, their condition is apparently incurable.

I find it interesting that the movie—and the book that inspired it—compared corporations to mentally ill people. Even if the comparison was damning, it was still apt in at least one way, because corporations, lest we lose sight of this fact, are composed of *people,* many of whom are in perfect mental health. And regardless of what the movie suggests, I believe that any entity made up of people is capable of positive change. Out of any organization composed of people comes social capital, a very valuable commodity these days. People's behaviour reflects their community's values. Presumably, people take those values with them to work every day. Sooner or later, there is bound to be a change for the better, if change is the will of the people.

That's the good news. The question is: How do we motivate the people running the corporations to make positive changes? How do we incorporate human values into our existing economic models?

Here's a thought. I've been saying for some time now that sustainability is like a train about to leave the station: the whistle is blowing, the doors are closing, get on board now or you're going to be left behind. I've always liked the sense of urgency that analogy creates, but I'm starting to think, more and more, that it really is true. And here's why.

As a group, as a social force, do you ever wonder whether corporations have gone too far?

It used to be that the Montreal Canadiens played at the Forum. Now they play at the Pepsi Forum. The Maple Leafs used to play at Maple Leaf Gardens, but now they play at the Air Canada Centre. In Ottawa, the Senators play at Scotiabank Place, formerly the Corel Centre. It used to be that in elementary schools, children were given free milk as a snack. Now schools in disadvantaged neighbourhoods raise extra funds by letting soft-drink companies put up advertising.

As a society, we used to think it made sense to protect very young children from being the targets of advertising campaigns. Now corporations are targeting children as young as two or three. According to a recent *Globe and Mail* article, in 1983 corporations spent $100 million U.S. on advertising to children age twelve and under. Today, they spend $15 *billion* U.S. The average child between the ages of eight and thirteen is exposed to some forty thousand commercials per year.

Everything on Earth is up for grabs, not just the minds and hearts of small children. Corporations are reaching into areas where they've never been permitted before. Everywhere you look, corporate money is running the show, from schools to prisons to ballparks to festivals. Corporations are patenting everything that goes by, from molecules to processes to DNA.

Of course, you know that I've made a career out of fund management—out of choosing stocks poised for growth, out of making money for investors. And I am still the chairman of HSBC Global Asset Management in Canada. So despite the rhetoric, I'm not really arguing against the notion of corporations making profits. Let's be honest. The whole point of being in business is to make money.

So what's my point? It's academic and speculative, and it's about a question. Considering the behaviour of corporations today, what's next? Where do we go from here?

The minds behind the movie *The Corporation* point out that, in the past 150 years, the corporation as we know it has evolved from being an almost insignificant entity in our society to being a pervasive omnipresence, an element you bump into everywhere you turn, a way of life—larger than life, even. It is our dominant social institution today, much as—the creators point out—the church, the monarchy and the Communist Party have been in other times and places.

But history, they argue, humbles dominant institutions. You only have to look at how much respect the monarchy gets these days to see how quickly change can happen. And as the moviemakers point out, all of these entities have been "crushed, belittled or absorbed into some new order... The corporation is unlikely to be the first to defy history."

I've been saying for some time now that I no longer believe infinite growth is possible given our limited natural resources, whether on a broad economic level or at the individual business level. Now I wonder if this idea can be expanded, figuratively, to include the corporate world more generally. That is, corporate North America cannot achieve limitless, infinite growth any more than its individual components, the companies themselves, can. Sooner or later, it will hit a ceiling, and something is going to have to change.

Call it an explosion, a spontaneous combustion, call it a rebirth—a new order will emerge. No entity that depends on people is eternally static, whether we're talking about a marriage, a friendship, a volunteer board of directors, a band of musicians or the people who make up corporations. In the same way that the cells in our bodies are constantly being renewed, all of these entities are continually in flux, moving to or from a new or an old state on their way to the next thing.

Metaphorically speaking, when corporations reach the pinnacle towards which they're headed, what will they do for their next act? When there is nothing else left on Earth that can be bought or sold, what shape will their next incarnation take? In what ways might the corporation as an entity substantially change or reinvent itself?

My guess and my hope is that the new drive will be towards sustainability.

Arguments over what should and should not be included in a definition of sustainability have been holding up the world's progress towards it. But I believe we are getting closer to a definition. I suggest that what we've been seeing is a convergence of certain values under the rubric of sustainability: social values, human values and environmental values. Taken together, they're what I'll refer to today as corporate social responsibility. I think corporate social responsibility is the new direction in which the best-run companies are heading. It's what people want. You don't have to look much further than the World Trade Organization protests to understand what's going on out there. And while you're looking at the protests, don't forget global telecommunications, the Internet, satellite TV and fibre optics. What happens virtually anywhere in the world can be depicted on your television or computer screen within minutes. Companies can be held responsible for their actions no matter where in the world they operate—and increasingly, they are being held responsible.

We live in a more skeptical, less trusting society than we did even as recently as fifty years ago. People take nothing at face value anymore. It's no longer good enough for corporations to say they're doing a good job. They have to prove it. They have to show it. It has to be witnessed. Corporations have to be transparent enough in their actions so that all of us can see them with our own eyes.

In the last few decades, and particularly the last few years, we've seen a groundswell of support develop everywhere in the world for socially and environmentally sustainable practices. We've seen anger, revulsion, outrage and protests in response to inhumane or environmentally damaging corporate practices, and that outrage has hurt some corporations' reputations and bottom lines.

There is more of this to come. Competition for market share is fierce, and consumers can choose from a wide selection of providers of just about anything, from cars to shoes to energy. Studies are showing that consumers with sufficient means will buy from socially responsible corporations even if their prices are slightly higher than those of competitors. If prices are equal, even more people will choose the responsible corporation over its more careless competitors.

Then there are investors, who are even more likely to be concerned about corporate social responsibility. Globalization has created a whole new set of liabilities for companies, and investors are keen to consider and mitigate those potential risks. There is a growing body of evidence to support the notion that socially responsible corporations are a better investment in the long run.

At its genesis, socially responsible investing was chiefly concerned with what we called "negative screening" to filter out the corporate bad boys. Over the years, this kind of investing has progressed to include looking at corporate accountability in the context of risk to long-term shareholder and stakeholder value. That's because a company's bottom line doesn't exist in a social vacuum. It's affected directly by shareholders, customers, employees, suppliers and communities, all of whom live in a world where value systems are always evolving. The corporation's value systems have to keep up.

For example, nobody used to care where their coffee came from as long as it was hot. In the past decade, there has been a coffee revolution. Information about fair trade, bird-friendly coffee; shade-grown coffee; and organic coffee, and news about the poor treatment and compensation of coffee farmers in developing countries, has created a huge market for purveyors of coffee with a conscience. That has resulted in the success stories we know of today as Starbucks and Bridgehead, among others.

Similarly, no one wants to find out that a company whose shoes they wear is relying on child labour in another country. No one wants to find out a company is dumping toxic effluent into the river they grew up swimming in. No one wants to find out the person who picked the banana they ate for breakfast later gave birth to a baby with defects because of the pesticides used. When people find out things like this, they vote with their wallets. They give their business to companies that are better behaved.

When corporations are discovered to be the perpetrators of environmental violations or worker exploitation, or are accused of unethical behaviour, consumers get hostile—and the smart investor is alarmed. The fact is that such misdemeanours are associated with poor management and flawed business models. The prudent investor knows these are the companies that will not improve their behaviour until expensive litigation or regulation forces them to. As a result, they will lag behind their competitors.

If you think about it, it only makes common sense that a well-run company should be socially responsible. Such companies are transparent, accountable for their business activities, responsive to shareholder concerns and communities. They establish best practices that raise the bar for their industries. Doesn't that sound like good management? Analysts are starting to think so. Conserving resources is also, obviously, good for the bottom line and so is thinking long term about the availability and management of resources.

An old acquaintance of mine, Deb Abbey, is the founder of Real Assets, the first investment management firm in Canada to focus exclusively on social investment. She manages portfolios for individuals and institutions across Canada and has written two books about social investing. When I asked for her point of view on corporate social responsibility and its link to profitability, she told me about a recent study that looked at the returns of socially screened mutual funds invested in Canadian equities. The study concluded that, on average, Canadian investors in socially screened mutual funds were not giving up anything in financial performance. In fact, the study concluded that social and environmental screens may decrease risk exposure in these portfolios. Explaining these findings, Deb points out that twenty years ago, financial statements reflected about 75 per cent of the true market value of major corporations. Today, according to Innovest Strategic Value Advisors, that number has plummeted to a trifling 15 per cent. The remaining 85 per cent of a company's value is based on management's perceived skill at handling intangibles such as brand equity, environmental liabilities, labour relations, customer partnerships and so on.

The issues we face as a global community today are vastly different from those we were concerned with twenty years ago. Now phrases such as climate change, human rights and ethical conduct are household words, and all of them can affect a company's bottom line if the company hasn't adequately considered and managed the risk involved. To address this, companies like Real Assets have developed processes that consider non-traditional risk when they select investments. Real Assets files shareholder resolutions that focus a company's attention on these issues and asks it to adopt policies and practices that provide increased transparency and accountability. These resolutions are a formal request for action, and votes on them are taken at companies' annual general meetings. Deb Abbey has filed resolutions on everything from corporate governance to human rights, climate change, responsible water use, the glass ceiling, HIV/AIDS and responsible finance. And she has seen positive changes.

The best-intentioned companies are becoming more aware of these risks to long-term shareholder value, because what looks like an intangible risk today can easily become a financial one tomorrow, especially in an environment where governments increasingly push liabilities back on private enterprise. A good example of this is Talisman Energy, whose share price dropped an estimated 15 per cent in response to shareholder pressure about its operations in Sudan. That happened because of inadequate risk analysis up front.

What I find really exciting is that Deb Abbey is not alone. In an address to the World Economic Forum in 1999, UN Secretary-General Kofi Annan challenged business leaders to join an international initiative called the Global Compact: a series of ten principles meant to bring companies together with UN agencies, labour and civil society on the subject of human rights, labour and the environment. Among other things, the principles ask that companies respect the protection of human rights and forbid human rights abuses; that they not use forced or child labour; that they consider the environment in all of their undertakings; and that they work against corruption, extortion and bribery.

To date, some 1,500 companies have signed on, and there are many major, influential investment companies among them. In fact, a total of twenty major investment firms endorsed the compact, among them such giants as Credit Suisse Group, Deutsche Bank, Morgan Stanley and Goldman Sachs. Together, these twenty firms control $6 *trillion* U.S. in assets.

That a collection of such powerful, dominant investment firms would endorse a set of explicit principles regarding sustainability is extremely compelling to me. It speaks volumes about where we're headed in the next few years. The twenty firms prepared a series of recommendations designed to better integrate environmental, social and governance issues into financial analysis and asset management. Their report, entitled *Who Cares Wins,* was issued at the Global Compact Leaders Summit in June, presented by Anthony Ling, a managing director at Goldman Sachs.

All you have to do is look at the names of the endorsing institutions on the report to be convinced that things are certainly going to change. The investment industry has arrived at the conclusion that environmental, social and governance issues are absolutely vital to a stable and healthy capital market—and, I would argue, to any company's survival in that market.

Corporations have not all caught up yet. There is still a gaping divide between what the investment community now recognizes as the gold standard and what the corporate world thinks the investment companies want. As Anthony Ling said when he presented the report, those of us fortunate enough to work in the financial markets are at the fulcrum between the corporate world and the providers of capital. We are in a unique position to understand the two worlds and help them meet. We can help to drive the process. And we will, because the reputation of our entire industry is at stake.

We would have more success if we had more support, however, and this brings me to some thoughts I'd like to close with.

I mentioned earlier that some 1,500 companies have signed the Global Compact, committing to its principles of sustainability. That's a large number, but significantly, the majority of those companies are not from North America. Why would that be? I think this is a shameful failing of our government. Other countries—including the U.S., Japan and most of Europe—have enacted more and better regulatory incentives that provide the demand companies need to design and market environmentally friendly products. Other countries are creating a context in which it makes good business sense to be sustainable. Other countries have been more proactive, more confident and less scared.

I'm not talking about stifling a free market, or replacing competition with regulation, or about handcuffing companies and strangling them with rules. But I do think Canada should show some leadership here. Incentives and regulations designed to encourage sustainability would help to shore up our economic foundation given the international business climate in which we all now operate. Meanwhile, we in the business world can busy ourselves with building a philosophical foundation to accompany the economic one. We can derive all the materials we need from community values. Sustainability has to be something all elements of society support, a grassroots sentiment with upward mobility fuelled by social capital. Not only can we minimize our use of resources, but we can aim for zero—and maybe even go beyond zero into repairing previous damage. We can recognize that the link between economics and sustainability is about reducing our cost of living, our cost of doing business and, ultimately, our footprint on the earth. This is the true element of conservation.

I'm often asked whether a company needs a visionary on board who can lead the charge, so to speak. My answer is that you don't. What you need is passion, and you need that passion to be infectious, so that everyone at the company, from the tall to the small, is equally invested in a personal way in the collective drive towards sustainability. People's behaviour reflects their community's values. Our economic models are not holistic, but they should be. They don't deal with human values, but they should. And one day at a time, with momentum that picks up every day, the corporate world is ensuring that someday they will, as the drive to become sustainable catches on.

My hope is that with this momentum will come a sense of purpose, that companies will find ways to get buy-in on sustainability from all of their employees, from the ground up. To succeed at being truly sustainable, a company needs to have a clear vision of itself as the best in its field, relative to its competition. But it also needs to foster that ambition in an absolute sense—it needs to want sustainability for its own sake, and it needs to determine a way to achieve it. Its employees need to understand and buy into the objectives to develop that all-important sense of purpose that will fuel the company's progress.

Ten years from now, I would like to look back at this speech and find that the people who made the movie *The Corporation* are planning a sequel—a documentary about the surprising corporate shift into sustainability, an investigation into how corporate North America accomplished a miraculous cure of itself, shedding its psychopathic persona and stepping into wiser, more ethical shoes. And how did the world change after that? Now that's a movie I'd like to see.

Thank you.

FOUR

All Change Begins with Dialogue

Totem pole by renowned Haisla artist Lyle Wilson.
A Christmas gift from Milton to his wife, Fei.

Raven and the Origin of Light
LYLE WILSON | 2000

Converting Ideas into Reality

ILTON WONG PUT forth many great ideas on how to make Vancouver, British Columbia, and Canada better. Lots of people have great ideas. Milton converted many of his ideas into reality. Quite a few people do realize their ideas, but where Milton found himself in very select company was when he exercised his ability to inspire other people to actually do the good work that his fertile and creative mind had determined needed to be done.

I first met Milton Wong in 1993. True to form, he was asking me to work with him to convert one of his ideas into reality. His goal was a strong, prosperous, culturally diverse Canada unencumbered by the myths and intolerance that have burdened so many societies.

One might imagine why Milton Wong would support such an idea. He was the son of immigrants, part of a "visible minority" for whom English was a second language. He grew up in a time when Canada was less open than it is now. However, Milton was not a victim. He acquired English and a good education, found work in the very conservative financial sector and went on start his own business and achieve great success. Milton's concern for others also led him to seek ways to improve openness and understanding in Canada. The vehicle to deliver his idea, in this case, was the Laurier Institution.

First, a note on the name. "Laurier" was chosen because Wilfrid Laurier was the first prime minister to welcome immigrants from many different countries to Canada. "Institution" was chosen because Wilfrid Laurier University in Waterloo, Ontario, already had a Laurier Institute. The purpose of the Laurier Institution is to encourage open discussion leading to a better, more tolerant Canada. To do this, the institution holds lectures, seminars and conferences and conducts research. It has published books and articles that are in use in educational institutions and elsewhere.

There are many reasons why I should never have allowed Milton to convince me to become involved with the Laurier. The pay was lousy. The supporting staff was almost non-existent. The tiny premises were dependent upon the good will of the landlord. (Milton at work again!) There was no obvious source of income beyond Milton's ability to twist arms and generate donations. The details of the institution's mandate and mission did not go beyond that one great idea.

So why did I agree to join the Laurier and serve as its executive director for ten years? First, who could turn down the chance to work towards such an important goal? Second, Milton never worked alone. Well before he approached me, he had assembled an amazing team of prominent, capable citizens to serve (for no pay!) as the board of directors of the Laurier, and they were sitting beside him when he made his pitch. Doing anything for Milton provided rich rewards in terms of the wonderful people you got to meet and work with.

Another reason to work with the Laurier Institution and Milton was the chance to make a positive difference with respect to First Nations. Our major effort in that direction was producing the book *Prospering Together: The Economic Impact of the Aboriginal Title Settlements in B.C.* The book sold out two editions and is still in use.

Milton Wong was a member of the Order of Canada. The order's motto is: "They desire a better country." Milton did more than desire a better Canada. He made it so.

Roslyn Kunin, *in addition to running the Laurier Institution, has taught at several Canadian universities, given frequent presentations and sat on and chaired many boards. She is in private practice as a consulting economist.*

The prize antique of Milton's father, Wong Kung Lai, this massive rug from a Buddhist monastary outside of Beijing depicts the empress dowager as a phoenix surrounded by a "court" of birds. Wong passed his passion for ancient Chinese culture on to his children.

On Important People

MILTON WONG BEGAN his first year as chancellor of Simon Fraser University in 1999, just as I was completing my last year as president. During that time, we did together what we both liked most about our jobs: sharing the stunning Arthur Erickson stage at convocation to greet and congratulate the hundreds of graduates who crossed the platform. There is no doubt in my mind that one of the most fitting appointments Milton ever accepted was the position as chancellor—first, for the opportunity to meet so many joyful people, and then, for the challenge, in a brief face-to-face moment, of signalling to each graduate something that might cap that precious instant in time.

In September 2000, Simon Fraser University opened the Morris J. Wosk Centre for Dialogue. For Milton, the Wosk Centre was like having a dream come true. He had by then clearly established himself as one of the city's leading gurus of dialogue and social innovation, and now he had, in the centre, the perfect place to play, as great professionals long to do. The centre's expressly designed space for dialogue was Asia Pacific Hall—a conversation space of five concentric circles providing uncommon natural light, great comfort, warm colours and the capacity for each participant to see the face of anyone who might speak. A feature Milton liked most was that there was no designated or obvious place for the chair, leader or whomever might see themselves as being "in charge." The design says that all participants are there as equals, a bedrock principle of dialogue. Milton loved it.

Not surprisingly, Milton took great pleasure in showing the Centre for Dialogue, particularly Asia Pacific Hall, to friends and visitors. After one such showing, he climbed the centre's perfect-piece-of-art staircase to the third floor to see the new office arrangement I shared with my assistant, Linda Kornik. He gently knocked then opened the door and introduced himself to Linda. From my office, I could hear the animated buzz, and I knew it was Milton. As I entered Linda's space, Milton turned to me and declared, "Jack, Linda and I were just talking about these bare walls"—arms extended like an eagle's wings—"and about how great these walls would look with art." After further discussion, Milton offered, should we wish, the loan of prints created by his sister Anna. He thought they would be perfect for our space and suggested a visit to his Cambie Street home, where some of Anna's work was stored. "You must come, too, Linda," Milton insisted. "This is your space, so you must make the final decision. But only if you like it, of course."

We agreed upon a date to see Anna's art. After Milton left, Linda said, "You know, Jack, when important people come to meet with you, most of them don't see me. It's like I am not even here." That was never the case with Milton.

On the appointed date, Milton graciously welcomed us to his home, proudly telling us that it had once been his parents' place. Family was so important to Milton, and he obviously took great pleasure in inviting Linda and me to see his sister's art. There were many beautiful framed prints to choose from, and we had fun conversing with Milton about art and life. Linda liked three pieces in particular.

These events took place more than ten years ago. Recently, I asked Linda what her thoughts were now on the loan-of-the-prints experience. Here is what she said:

Milton's ability to connect and match those in need with those who can provide extended to our own little office. He intuitively knew that his sister's prints would be a perfect fit for the office. Instead of just bringing in the art as a done deal, he was sensitive enough to ask for our input—especially mine, since I would be working in the immediate area—and so gracious to invite me to his home to select what I might like. I was very touched. His actions were based on dialogue: an ability to see everyone as an individual, his understanding that everyone's preferences would differ and his respect for those differences.

Thank you, Linda. Thank you, Milton.

Jack Blaney *is president emeritus, Simon Fraser University.*

ANN COWAN

Panarchy
Rules

O UR PATHS CROSSED at Simon Fraser University. Milton Wong was our new chancellor, a role he took seriously and approached with enormous energy and creativity. Milton realized immediately that the Wosk Centre for Dialogue could be a powerful agent of change and a safe environment for difficult conversations on vexing issues. And he had a long list of vexing issues: environmental sustainability, aquaculture, Aboriginal land claims, human rights, health care (in the broadest sense of the term), social housing, Aboriginal education and governance, funding for the arts and so on. It didn't take him long to seek me out as a partner in his concerns, nor did it take me more than a nanosecond to realize what a resource we had in Milton.

I had recently become the director of programs at the Morris J. Wosk Centre for Dialogue, a position funded by the North Growth Management Foundation. As I focussed on what kinds of programs would define our new centre, I was mindful of the responsibility to fulfill the faith in dialogue as an instrument of social change that had inspired forward-thinking community leaders to join with SFU in this experiment. When I think back over our years of "sparking," I realize that Milton and I rarely had a formal meeting. Of course there were many meetings with others, which Milton often asked me to arrange, but in our case he would just show up. He would phone me to say, "I'm two blocks from you, what are you doing?" or appear in my doorway and say, "Walk with me to my next meeting." Or there would be a call: "I'm on my way to Hong Kong. Have you got a minute to talk?"

127

One day, Milton called from the Centre for Dialogue to say he wanted to explain an idea that could serve as a framework for addressing those vexing issues. When I arrived, he was sitting alone in Asia Pacific Hall as the delegates filtered out, making diagrams on the back of his program. He wanted me to understand "panarchy." He was vibrating with excitement: someone had created a theory that made sense of what he had intuitively understood and practised all his life.

If you Google "panarchy," you will discover that "archy" means government and "pan" suggests all-embracing. So panarchy, as it is used by social theorists, is an idea that posits the interconnectedness of human actions and natural occurrences and shows how these interact in a looping way. Milton's diagram looked like a figure eight. He explained that all human endeavours move forward towards order and stability as they are achieved; at the same time, they are vulnerable to creating disturbance, caused sometimes by the effect of their forward action. This disturbance results in a back loop, during which there is creative disorganization, reorganization and reconfiguration—all of which can lead to innovation. A pessimist might say, "Nothing good will come of good" or, in the words of the poet Robert Frost, "Nothing gold can stay." An optimist might say, "The backward loop is our biggest opportunity." You can guess what Milton's response was!

The Centre for Dialogue opened not long before the events of September 11, 2001. That was followed by the SARS epidemic, prompting waves of uncertainty that affected our projections for activity at the centre in our crucial early years. But here was our greatest opportunity, claimed Milton—the world was in a period of reorganization and innovation, and the Wosk Centre and Simon Fraser University would be at the heart of it.

Of course, Milton went on to delve much more deeply into the ideas outlined by C.S. Holling and Lance Gunderson in their book, *Panarchy: Understanding Transformations in Human and Natural Systems.* He invited a few core participants to a meeting with C.S. Holling, known as Buzz, and renowned social innovation scholar Frances Westley to stimulate dialogue among faculty and graduate students. This was followed by a daylong workshop on panarchy and social innovation. The focus was on turning ideas into practical solutions, always Milton's priority. "How can we make this happen?" he would say.

This story illustrates how excited Milton was by new thinking and how eager he was to learn more and to inspire his colleagues with ideas. It also shows how widely Milton cast his net. As chancellor of SFU, he held the most senior, albeit ceremonial, position in the university, yet he counted among his colleagues everyone he worked with, regardless of their status. His annual Christmas party was a testament to his inclusiveness. The highlight, in addition to his family's wonderful cooking, was a competitive present-passing game that allowed for some friendly score-settling, since you could seize an unwrapped gift from a colleague (including a superior) rather than choosing a wrapped surprise. Milton liked to play, but he was never frivolous: his work, life, family and professional and private pursuits were all part of a panarchic piece.

I learned a lot from Milton about how to do my job and how to live my life, but he was very sly. Every conversation began with "I need your help" or "I need your ideas" or "I need your advice" or "Can you sort this out for me?" Of course, this was his way of giving me advice or sorting me out, but he got me every time.

The writer Maya Angelou said: "I've learned that people will forget what you said, people will forget what you did, but people will never forget how you made them feel." Milton Wong sparked social innovation through his ideas, his cheerleading and his strategic partnerships and investments. But it was the way he made people feel that made all the difference.

Ann Cowan worked at Simon Fraser University for thirty-four years in many capacities, ending her career there as executive director of the Vancouver campus. Milton and Fei Wong were inspiring mentors and compassionate friends.

Milton's older sister, Anna Wong, had become a renowned professional artist, whose work was recognized nationally and internationally for bringing together her Chinese ancestry and her contemporary Western art education. Anna had a tremendous influence on Milton.

Some of her later work was inspired by visits to China, sometimes taken with Milton. In this piece, Anna combined images of the ancestral birthplace of Confucius and the Wong family ancestral home in rural Guangdong. Milton was a strong supporter of Anna and her career as a professional artist. After Anna retired from exhibiting and producing work, he purchased her remaining collection and displayed her work in his office.

Confucius's Birthplace
ANNA WONG | 1985

STEPHEN J. TOOPE

In Praise
of Enthusiasm

MILTON WONG WAS an enthusiastic human being. "An enthusiastic human being": in Milton's case, each word of that simple description carries great import.

Milt's being was infused with energy, drive and commitment. I remember the first time I met him, in 2003. I had just become president of the Trudeau Foundation, and I was reporting to my first board meeting. Milton was a board member. I had read up on him and was of course impressed by his distinguished career. I had met and worked with lots of big-business types but, I soon discovered, none like Milton. The moment he opened his mouth, I encountered a being with almost supernatural optimism, a being who was always thinking about the big questions in life, a being who wanted to make our society, our country and the world better—and who actually had ideas about how we just might do it.

Oh, those ideas! Some people thought of Milton as a serial entrepreneur, and he was. But he was every bit as much a serial social innovator. From dragon boat festivals to economic development in Aboriginal communities, from the promotion of sustainable development to the creation of unparalleled opportunities for intercultural dialogue through Simon Fraser University and the Laurier Institution, Milton was a seeder of positive change. His very being exuded hope and promise.

Milt's humanity expressed itself in concern for the welfare of people of all creeds, colours and conditions. Of course, that made him a great philanthropist. All across the province, especially here in Vancouver, we have benefited

MILTON was a seeder of

positive change. His very being

exuded hope and promise.

as a society from his and Fei's generosity. But humanity is not about writing cheques. When Milton was concerned about an issue, he got involved directly and very personally. He brought people together.

One day, I briefly mentioned to him that I wanted to help UBC become a focus for dialogue across cultures. A few weeks later, Milt asked whether he and Fei could host an event at my house, where the young pianist Avan Yu would play. The Wongs had bid for this prize at a charity auction. It sounded fun, and my wife, Paula, and I happily agreed. When the day arrived, we discovered that the guests were a constellation of the brightest and most committed young intercultural activists in Vancouver. I had to laugh, because I knew Milton was gently challenging me. He was saying, "So, if you are serious, these are the people you need to listen to." That was Milt, a connector par excellence but a humanist who wanted people to challenge each other to do better.

And all of this social action and human connecting was conducted with such enthusiasm. Milt was a good man but not a smug one, not someone who took everything too seriously. Oh, that wide smile and that hearty laugh! And he could be pretty darn competitive. One misty day, my family was visiting the Wongs at their beautiful Taku retreat on Quadra Island. My son, thirteen or so at the time, challenged Milton to a game of tennis. Not wanting to miss a single opportunity to score a point against this young boy, Milt crashed into the net. At first I thought, "Why does he care so much?" But having come to know Milton, I realized that it was not just his competitive streak; it was his fundamental belief that learning takes place everywhere and all the time. He wanted to show my son that doing something well—and with enthusiasm—matters, even if it is just a game of tennis.

I said earlier that Milton always wanted to make our society, our country and the world better. He did.

Stephen J. Toope was named the twelfth president and vice-chancellor of the University of British Columbia on March 22, 2006. He began his second five-year term in July 2011. Professor Toope is active in many associations, currently serving as chair of the Association of Universities and Colleges of Canada (AUCC), member of the Research Council of the Canadian Institute for Advanced Research (CIFAR) and member of the board of directors for the Public Policy Forum.

A Constant
Source of Inspiration

"DO YOU KNOW that you and I are both related to this plant?" exclaimed Milton Wong one afternoon, pointing towards the flowering peace lily in the corner of my office.

Milton had just sat in on an undergraduate biology lecture and, fascinated with what he had learned, had a passion to share it. I was then a vice-president at Simon Fraser University and had encouraged Milton to allow his name to stand as a candidate for chancellor. Now that he was serving in that capacity, the university was discovering a different kind of leadership. Not only did Milton epitomize the kind of community engagement that any university aspires towards, but he was also intellectually engaged with the institution, intensely curious about its teaching and research activities. This provided healthy doses of inspiration to students, faculty and staff. I already knew Milton as an extraordinary and far-sighted business leader with a strong social conscience. While he was chancellor, I had the opportunity to get to know him better. And that had a profound impact on my life.

Milton Wong was a humble man who likely underestimated the influence he exerted on friends and associates. Nevertheless, the powerful combination of his wisdom and his irrepressible optimism permeated most of his relationships. Far better than most, Milton understood that diversity is a source of strength, that innovation requires risk-taking and that values underpin all of the successes in our business and personal lives. Almost a generation ago, he was the first prominent business leader in British Columbia to call for a resolution of Aboriginal land claims, not only because it would boost investment in the province, but because it was a matter of social justice. It was the right thing to do.

At SFU, Milton was especially engaged with the continuing development of the university's downtown Vancouver campus. Fascinated by the Wosk Centre for Dialogue, he probably logged more hours in the circular Asia Pacific Hall than anyone else, exploring different kinds of leadership models and new ways of discussing policies and ideas. He also helped spearhead efforts to ensure that the university's School for the Contemporary Arts was part of the solution for the repurposed Woodward's site in Vancouver's Downtown Eastside. This heritage restoration and redevelopment was very close to Milton's heart, as he grew up only blocks away on the edge of Chinatown. And it is fitting that the Fei and Milton Wong Experimental Theatre is now a centre of this vibrant cultural precinct.

Milton served as chancellor of SFU from 1999 to 2005, during which time his positive impact was deeply felt. His loyalty to the university continued after that, even as he continued his active involvement in numerous other enterprises, national associations and community activities.

In 2002, I moved to Ottawa, accepting a position as vice-president of the University of Ottawa. Milton would call on his occasional visits to the national capital to share breakfast or dinner and get caught up. He always had new business ideas he was working on and young entrepreneurs he was encouraging and supporting. His passion for making a difference in the world grew every year, becoming increasingly infectious for all those who knew and admired him. And, of course, we would talk politics, too, for Milton was always fascinated by public life. A number of political parties, federal and provincial, attempted to recruit him to run for office over the years. However, Milton always knew his own mind, understanding that he was engaged in public service of a different kind.

One of his remarkable characteristics was his constancy. Milton was always Milton. Regardless of whether he was in a corporate boardroom, a public meeting, a community function or a private conversation, he presented the same focussed curiosity and broad perspective. His uncontainable smile, however, was probably most evident when he was cooking a sumptuous meal for friends in his Vancouver home or relaxing with Fei and other members of his family at their beloved Taku resort on Quadra Island.

In 2009, I was offered the position of president and CEO of the Public Policy Forum. When I called Milton to let him know I was considering the move, he offered encouragement, suggesting the job would give me the opportunity to make a bigger contribution to the country. He knew the Public Policy Forum, which had honoured him in 2002 at one of its Testimonial Dinner & Awards nights in Toronto—one of the many, many awards he received in his lifetime. Milton was recognized on that occasion for his leadership in promoting good governance and sound public policy in Canada.

Milton Wong's unique brand of leadership offered vivid proof that life is all about relationships. Time and again, Milton's successes amply demonstrated this truism. As a businessman, venture capitalist, angel investor, community leader, philanthropist, social activist, university chancellor, mentor, friend and family man, Milton consistently showed us why trust is such a precious commodity, one that must be carefully nurtured in all of our relationships. That's how he inspired us.

David Mitchell *is president and* CEO *of Canada's Public Policy Forum. He is an author and commentator, who has served as an executive in B.C.'s resource industries, as an elected member of the B.C. legislature and as a vice-president of three Canadian universities: Simon Fraser University, the University of Ottawa and Queen's University.*

This painting by Anna Wong depicts

the famous Dun Huang Caves in China.

After China's opening and reform,

Milton often travelled there on

business and remained fascinated by

the country's dynamism and stunning

economic transformation.

(along the silk road)   Hana Wong

MILTON K. WONG

Harnessing the Power of Collaboration: Taking Aboriginal Businesses to the Next Level

KEYNOTE ADDRESS TO THE CANADIAN COUNCIL
FOR ABORIGINAL BUSINESS 6TH ANNUAL
VANCOUVER GALA DINNER, SEPTEMBER 30, 2008

GOOD EVENING.

First of all, I wish to acknowledge that we are meeting here on the traditional territory of the Coast Salish people. I would also like to recognize Chief Shawn Atleo, who was recently appointed chancellor of Vancouver Island University.

I see a disparity between the potential of Aboriginal businesses to succeed, on the one hand, and the likelihood of their success, on the other. There is a gap—and I believe collaboration is one way to bridge it. That was going to be the theme of my address today: the role of collaboration in business, including why it's important, how it works and even how it can enrich your cultural identity.

And then the global financial meltdown happened. As we will see in a moment, massive global collaboration was partly behind the turmoil, so it seems to me that not discussing it would be ignoring the elephant in the room. After all, I represent a global bank, and you are business people, and the crisis has coloured everything for investors and business people alike lately.

So I've gone back to the drawing board to consider collaboration in the context of the global capital markets. My plan now is to talk about the crisis first, and then offer some understanding of what it means for businesses like yours as you wrestle with the notion of collaboration in the age of globalization.

The financial turbulence going on right now is really indicative of inter-connected business activity around the world. It was ignited when U.S. banks began offering incentives to tempt more customers to take out subprime loans. With house prices rising, and easy initial terms, many people took on mortgages that were much bigger than they could comfortably afford. Large, high-ratio mortgages were extended to people with low incomes and poor credit histories. Borrowers assumed they would be able to refinance quickly at more favourable terms. But then housing prices started to drop. Refinancing became difficult, if not impossible. People began to default on their mortgages. Interest rates climbed, and the number of foreclosures escalated swiftly. Eventually, the rising number of foreclosures triggered the collapse that's been making headlines since mid-September.

But how did U.S. bank loans become a global problem? The U.S. housing crisis was amplified by too much mortgage and other debt, much of it bad. Those debts were bundled together and sold to financial institutions, backed by collateral in the U.S. housing market. A significant chunk of this debt was being held by financial institutions around the world. Eventually, they began to crumble.

This is an example of collaboration on a colossal scale. Just look at the players involved: from first-time homeowners to American banks to distributors to global financial institutions and their clients. You can envision it as a spiderweb, with U.S. consumers at the centre, far-flung economies at the periphery and everybody else in between—all connected.

It's true enough that not all players were in this game deliberately, in the real sense of the word "collaboration," but each played an important role in a large, intricately related system that depends on the involvement of multiple stakeholders to function properly. When one part of the system began to malfunction, it was difficult to contain the problem.

This is a state of affairs that would have been unthinkable just a generation or two ago. In the old days, businesses could operate successfully without collaborating at all. Before roads, before cars, before telephones, computers and the Internet, before globalization, it was easier to be self-sufficient. Business people kept their noses clean and went about running their shops and services independently. For one thing, there was less to know. You could specialize in a dozen different areas, because the amount of knowledge available to the average person was smaller and easier to master.

I think it's fair to say that this is the stage where many Aboriginal businesses remain today. There may be thousands of joint ventures going on, which is great, but many of them are indeed localized in the manner I just described.

Contrast that to where the greater world has been heading.

The word "multinational" wasn't even coined until about 1960. But since then, we've been living in a world where the need to specialize—and rely on other specialists—has grown ever more apparent. It's much harder now to operate your business as an island unto itself. In this era of globalization and technology, you need suppliers, partners, allies and collaborators—and, yes, you even need your competitors. The increasingly complex demands that globalization and technology are placing on the resources, services, skills and knowledge that businesses can offer require more collaborative ventures. The very nature of competition in business has changed.

American author Gore Vidal once wrote, "It is not enough to succeed. Others must fail." Does that sound familiar? This attitude once characterized the business world. But today, a business that initiates a war by bringing this attitude to the game may be headed for failure. The airline industry is a good example. By trying to drive each other out of business through price wars, airlines have made it much more difficult for themselves to make profits. The idea is not to get in bed with a direct competitor, of course, but rather to court another business that complements yours and devise mutually agreeable terms that help both of you get ahead.

Now you may be thinking: Isn't that exactly what American consumers, banks and investment firms were doing when the financial crisis exploded? And true enough, the capital markets themselves are a huge collaboration. So why am I standing here promoting collaboration if a widespread crisis like this is what can come of it?

There are certain conditions that make collaboration effective, and the current financial crisis occurred in the absence of those required conditions. The missing key ingredient was common moral sentiment among the collaborators. From the hapless homeowners who couldn't even afford a down payment to the denizens of Wall Street and on to the banks of the world, the various players were not working from the same book of rules when they joined the game.

The term "common moral sentiment" was originally coined by Adam Smith, an economist and philosopher best known for his book on free trade and market economics, *The Wealth of Nations,* first published back in 1776. Smith is credited with creating the foundation of our modern belief that a free market cannot function properly without a set of established common social values and practices to which people and businesses adhere. What really strikes me is that Smith had written a treatise on moral sentiment nearly twenty years before he wrote *The Wealth of Nations.* In other words, although he was talking about free markets, he had already explored the idea of a common moral sentiment in doing business. That's how important he thought it was.

Smith also said he would choose a partnership over a corporation any day, because he knew that his partner's moral sentiments were important in a business relationship. That's a very important point. It speaks to the notion that a corporation, as an entity, is essentially amoral by nature. It doesn't spontaneously generate values. So rather than expecting corporations to generate a moral sentiment, it is necessary to create the principles and invite voluntary participation.

As they say, there is honour among thieves: even if you do business with crooks, it's best to have a shared understanding of the values and principles by which you're going to operate. Even Tony Soprano had his standards.

But let's turn our attention back to the good guys. When you live in a democracy where people look out for each other's well-being, you need a common moral sentiment so that people can trust each other. That trust becomes a powerful basis for moving forward socially, politically and in business. Let's take the World Trade Organization Ministerial Conference of 1999 as an example. Some of you may recall the Seattle riots of that year—sometimes known as the Battle of Seattle—when business people around the world woke up and said, "Wait a minute, why are people mad at us?" It was because corporate behaviour was out of step with evolving public values on environmental and other issues, such as labour conditions in Third World countries. Corporations at that time had still not learned from Enron; they were letting market forces dictate prices and responding accordingly. Through greed, they had been able to take advantage of the system. Then they were shocked by the massive street protests that erupted in Seattle. They didn't know what hit them.

Of course, people were protesting corporations' amoral behaviour. Now compare and contrast: Ten years later, we have the beginnings of a common moral sentiment in the UN Global Compact.

The compact was launched when Kofi Annan, then Secretary-General of the United Nations, asked all corporations to voluntarily abide by ten key principles that focus on social and environmental values as well as human rights and ethical business practices. The ten principles were established with insights from international labour organizations, and today nearly four thousand major corporations have joined the compact, which is the world's largest voluntary corporate responsibility initiative.

The companies that have joined come from all over the world, operate in dozens of different languages, have any number of different corporate cultures, come in all sizes and shapes and sell a wide variety of products or services. Yet they've all promised to be guided by the ten principles set out in the compact, because they can agree on this particular set of values. And because so many companies have signed on, the movement towards sustainability and corporate social responsibility continues to gain momentum.

But a compact like this only works if you believe in it. Compliance has to be voluntary, and it has to be good for a company's bottom line.

This is a far different state of affairs from the bad old days of Enron, when corporations had no collective conscience or shared sense of values—no common moral sentiment. The bottom line, it turns out, is that to function properly, capitalism is a system that requires a moral framework.

So how does that happen? The government's role is to make the rules and enforce them; the private sector's job is to abide by them. This is my own simplification of a position advanced by the late writer and activist Jane Jacobs in a favourite book of mine called *Systems of Survival.* The central idea is that in modern society, the government and the business world have very different roles to play within our moral system. The government creates regulations and enforces them, acting as the police, and businesses rely on those rules and regulations as they go about their operations. Although each of these worlds turns on a different set of rules, we don't run into problems unless the two collide. Conflict arises when collusion begins to take place.

To state it more simply, when government and business begin to have shared interest, without a clear separation, trouble begins to brew. What you should take from this first part of my talk is this one message: Collaboration works—indeed it is necessary in the age of globalization—but it must be based on a common moral sentiment.

AS MANY OF you know, I have been involved for many years with the developments of the Haisla Nation in Kitimat. As a result, I am keenly aware of the economic, political and social barriers that stand in the way of progress. In case you think I'm wearing rose-tinted glasses here, I want to say I realize that:

· Past attempts to engage First Nations in economic development have failed because you weren't at the table when programs were designed.
· Your bands are dealing with chronic unemployment as well as educational and social issues that may make business development difficult—after all, you need qualified people to perform essential business functions. This is a very large capacity-building problem.

· Access to capital has been a major obstacle to First Nations economic development, and so has a lack of understanding of how to acquire, manage and assess debt. The same goes for equity ownership.

This is just a short list, of course. As you may know all too well, there are other impediments. So I'm certainly not going to insist that collaboration is simple and that by using it you can change the fortunes of Aboriginal people overnight. But I also know you are looking for a fresh, strategic approach to old problems, and I think collaboration is at least part of the solution.

To see what you stand to gain by it, let's consider some interesting business facts—first about the Canadian economy in general, and then about the potential for Aboriginal businesses in particular. I think this will give you a reasonable sense of the opportunities that are out there and a feeling that some of the obstacles are surmountable after all.

First, the big picture: As a nation, Canada seems to be avoiding most of the major pitfalls and issues that are plaguing the United States. In good part, that's because our institutions have been very strong in terms of moral sentiment. Our central bank under people like David Dodge has been able to provide the necessary moral suasion to keep our financial system intact. That strong leadership has minimized any ill-advised behaviour. Our banking system is one of the best in the world.

BESIDES THAT, WE are well served by the fact that Canada is known as a nation of resources. And although it's true that we have natural resources in abundance, the fact is that they are limited. And when any resource is in limited supply, competition for that resource increases. In that context, consider that:

· The emerging large middle classes in developing countries such as Brazil, Russia, India and China will be key drivers behind the world's consumption of resources. The middle class in China, for example, is now 300 million strong—not far from the size of the entire United States. That's a lot of demand for our natural resources.

· Regardless of which president Americans elect this fall, the United States will move towards energy self-sufficiency, and Canada's tar sands will play a major role. For years to come, there will be major capital expansion in this sector as we build the infrastructure needed to transport resources to China and the U.S.

· As a nation of just 33 million people, our exports account for about 40 per cent of our GDP. And as a nation composed of people from so many different countries, our trade relations are significantly enhanced. These facts speak to our status as a favoured nation. We are connected economically throughout the world, and a combination of factors makes us privileged, including our banking system; our minimal deficit; and our reputation for discipline, values and trustworthiness. All of these points will augur well for us. Moral sentiment will play a role here. There will be significant business opportunities for you to take advantage of.

So those are the big-picture advantages. Now let's look at local advantages. Consider that Aboriginal people influence 20 per cent of Canada's land mass, a figure that is expected to rise to 30 per cent in the next fifteen years. And there are already more than 27,000 Aboriginal-owned businesses in Canada. Also working for you is the fact that the Aboriginal sector is growing in educational and employment capacity, technical skills, purchasing power and control over land and resources.

It's impossible not to look at these two key facts side by side—Aboriginal ownership of and influence on so much rich land, on the one hand, and the projected demand for resources that I just outlined, on the other—and not be struck by the potential.

In fact, collaboration is a business idea that makes even better sense in light of the world's recent recognition that natural resources are finite. When any resource is dwindling or in limited supply, competition for that resource increases. You have influence over 20 per cent of Canada's land mass. That seems to bode very well for you. But you will not be able to monetize that value without collaboration.

So perhaps we can view the current financial crisis as an opportunity for Aboriginals, looking ahead. Let's think about how you can participate in the markets more fully. First of all, I would ask: Can you collaborate with each other? Can you collaborate with universities? With provincial governments? With corporations?

The answer in all cases should be yes. If you can develop a common moral sentiment, where your values, goals and objectives are aligned, you can develop relationships that are, simply stated, win-win situations.

I've spoken in broad terms about why collaboration is critical. Now I'll get more specific about why it's important and touch on how to get started:

· Collaboration leads to the sharing of ideas. Finding out what other groups are doing or working towards, what their strengths and specialties are, can help you take a business idea to the next level.
· Collaboration can broaden your knowledge base, sharpen your market intelligence and lead you to identify opportunities and strategic alliances you might not have encountered otherwise.
· Collaboration makes it easier for your business to acquire competencies it would otherwise lack.

For example, when a small firm teams up with a big one, the smaller one gains access to economies of scale and the reach of the large company, while the large company benefits from access to greater innovation.

Now, for collaboration to happen, someone needs to take the first step and initiate a dialogue. I suggest you begin by working together to develop a community compact of common values and basic principles. Only if you do that can you begin to make a difference—and not just economically but in terms of health care, education and many other social and political areas.

It's also important to understand that when you develop a compact, those who are collaborating with you will know what your values are. When you seek partnerships, others will be fully aware of your objectives, which can hasten your ability to make the deals you want.

Whether the goal is better health care or education, combating racism or raising awareness, fighting pollution, promoting knowledge of native culture and arts or pursuing land claims, you will get ahead faster and be more effective if you share knowledge and build consensus through collaboration.

Right here in B.C., there are more than two hundred bands and 170,000 Aboriginals. So maybe a good place to begin today is to contemplate how you would manage collaboration among people at a social level. Collaboration is not just a business strategy but can be applied in any area where you need development.

For example, if you and I were going to do business together, I would ask: What are some of the social principles that we both want to follow? Social, political and commercial collaboration are all connected, because the values you espouse as a business are grounded originally in how you conduct yourself as a person, both socially and politically.

Moving from the social arena to the political, with regards to collaborating with the broader community, you are already on solid ground. We are fortunate in Canada to have strong Supreme Court judgements that have protected Aboriginal peoples' inherent rights by confirming the need for consultation and accommodation. That has set a positive tone for future relationships. Corporations now know the rules of engagement, and this lends a valuable element of certainty to the deals you want to make.

Certainty is a core motivating factor for people looking to make deals with Aboriginals. Given what has been defined by the Supreme Court—and considering the fact that there is a need for major capital expenditures where assets will be sited on territories—the most compelling drive for collaboration by the outside world is the need for certainty on major capital projects.

For example, consider the relationship of Rio Tinto Alcan with the Haisla Nation. Through the Rio Tinto Alcan–Haisla protocol, under the guidance and visionary leadership of Chief Steve Wilson, the Haisla actively supported a $2 billion project to take place on their territory. Also thanks largely to Steve Wilson, a $10 million foundation was set up for the purpose of capacity building, and there will be accommodation in terms of economic and commercial relations between the Haisla and Rio Tinto Alcan on issues such as procurement.

For another example of the price of certainty, consider the reluctance of major electric utilities to agree to the purchase of wood pellets for sale to Japan. We are keenly aware, for example, that to have twenty-year contracts selling wood pellets to Japan, a company must be able to assure delivery of the product over the long term. Or if we are to cement multi-billion dollar investments in a pipeline that cuts across Aboriginal territory, we have to show certainty that there will not be disruptions over long periods of time.

This is a powerful way for Aboriginals to become business partners, because businesses know that certainty is what they need to create economic entities that will withstand the rigours of time. And only you can offer it.

That's why I feel you have so much to gain by embracing this brand of collaboration. Consider the differences between a partnership and a master-servant relationship. A true partnership involves ownership. Partners have common goals, and both sides lose when things go badly. Their shared interest in the success of a venture forces them to recognize each other's worth. Aboriginal partnerships can bring something significant to the table—not pipeline expertise, necessarily, but certainty of delivery of the product over a long period of time. Their involvement may offer welcome reassurance that someone will be looking out for the investment—a guardian on the land acting as a safeguard.

I'm speaking from personal experience on this. I have the privilege of having become part of the Haisla Nation. I have been engaged with them through my voluntary work with Rio Tinto Alcan, building capacity for this small band. That work has given me the insight I needed to give this speech. I can see the issues involved from the perspective of the Haisla, from the perspective of Rio Tinto Alcan, from my perspective as an investment professional and from my perspective as someone who keeps track of the world market for natural resources.

And I see a fascinating confluence of these variables happening. For example, Chief Steve Wilson has talked about a half-mile energy corridor between the border of the province of Alberta and the waters of Douglas Channel. The need for this would be driven by the pure economics involved in getting Canada's resources to world markets. This is the vision that Chief Wilson has.

What's especially interesting to me about this idea is that there are fourteen Aboriginal bands in that corridor that need to be accommodated. That fact has caused us to look at concepts like that of an Aboriginal Crown corporation, whereby the interests of Aboriginal communities would be protected and Aboriginal partners would have equity ownership. For now it's just an idea—and, of course, negotiations would have to take place—but I believe the concept is valid. Through collaboration of this magnitude, Aboriginals will collectively get value out of their land.

I'd like to conclude by pointing out that even though treaty negotiations are ongoing, there is nothing stopping the Aboriginal business community from moving directly, concurrently, into business relationships.

And I encourage you to mentor your young leaders. According to the Canadian Council for Aboriginal Business, Aboriginal people are the fastest-growing segment of the Canadian population, and half are under the age of twenty-five. That's a lot of young potential. Existing Aboriginal leaders should, as part of their responsibilities, play an active role in building the younger generation. It's very important, if you're building collaboration on projects that are going to last twenty years or more, to demonstrate your capacity to retain those relationships. You will need your younger people to be ready to be meaningful partners. They are an essential part of the process as you begin to harness the power of collaboration in today's business world.

Meetings such as today's are essential for the kind of networking that is the beginning of collaboration. Allow me to end my presentation now, so you can continue to network and begin to collaborate.

Thank you.

FIVE

We're All in This Together

Drawn to the abstract nature of the piece, Milton
purchased this painting at an opening at Equinox Gallery.

Pond AE II
GORDON SMITH | 1996

Milton Wong,
Inveterate Bridge Builder

MY FIRST ENCOUNTER with Milton Wong was in the context of Science World and, from there, the Laurier Institution. It quickly became apparent that we shared common values and aspirations. This created a platform for us to engage more broadly, and Milt became interested in the work of the Aga Khan Foundation, with which I was very involved. AKF was a new dimension for Milt, and with his usual intellectual curiosity, he wanted to learn more. The foundation's philosophy of placing the individual at the centre of development, and our trust in people to change their own environment, resonated deeply with him. Faith in the resilience of the human spirit to overcome great odds when provided the wherewithal was a hallmark of his own life's work. Milt met Firoz Rasul and other colleagues also involved with AKF, leading in 2000 to his joining the national committee of Aga Khan Foundation Canada, on which he served with distinction for ten years.

Milt's ability to see things from all perspectives—that of beneficiaries in the developing world as well as of AKFC's stakeholders, supporters and donors—was unique. Khalil Shariff, the CEO of AKFC, remembers that Milt was "amazingly astute, empathetic and sensitive, forever able, in his inimitably disarming yet piercing way, to ask just the right question keeping the focus on the human element." True to form, Milt brought AKFC into conversations and collaborations with wider constituencies. As Khalil Shariff recalls, Milt "cut across all types of boundaries and ostensible dichotomies, continuously and effortlessly straddling if not dissolving them."

The catalytic role that Milt played in bringing people together to change things for the better, and his profound sense of shared citizenship, deepened our friendship. It also led to our working together on other endeavours and having amazing conversations about our country—Canada. Milt was a role model, a success story of someone who had bridged the immigrant divide but understood it. The Vancouver of thirty years ago was a different scene, relatively closed, uncertain and even suspicious of newcomers. Milton saw the urgent need for promoting mutual understanding and respect if the arrival of new immigrants and refugees wasn't going to strain social cohesion in a rapidly changing city. As a passionate bridge builder, he strove to build a better Canada, one enriched by its diversity but cemented by the shared responsibilities of citizenship.

Milt was impressed and in a way fascinated by his encounter with members of the Ismaili community, which he generously ascribed to beginning with our meeting. With his genuine desire to learn, he took it upon himself to understand what made the community tick. Most of its members had come to Vancouver after the forced expulsion from Uganda by Idi Amin. Milt was struck, as he often said, by the community's resourcefulness, self-reliance, adaptability and work ethic, as well as the strong volunteer ethos that guides our interactions and behaviour. It was these characteristics that Milt saw as the ingredients for the Ismaili community's successful integration into the larger Vancouver community in a relatively short period. He was very excited about my appointment in 1989 as deputy chair and in 1992 as chair of Canada's Immigration and Refugee Board, the country's largest tribunal, a mandate I fulfilled for eight years under two federal governments. Milt often spoke of this as an example of what Canada represented: that I, as an immigrant woman from B.C., could strive for and attain high public office. Once I moved to Ottawa, our discussions on the tension between Canadian values as embodied in the Canadian constitution and public perception became more focussed. This was a period during which immigration and refugee issues became highly charged, with concerns over levels of immigration and what some considered an ill-conceived open-door policy for refugees. Milt recognized the knowledge gap that often contributes to misunderstanding and even hostility towards the "other."

Milt was fascinated by His Highness the Aga Khan's definition of pluralism as "a prerequisite for development," essential to "the very survival of an interdependent world." Milt felt honoured that His Highness had chosen Canada as the home of the Global Centre for Pluralism, a partnership between the Aga Khan Development Network and the Canadian government. Milt was one of the early contributors to the thinking around the creation of the GCP, and the concept was in keeping with his expansive view of Canadian diversity. Firoz Rasul recalls Milt's invaluable role as a sounding board and the wise counsel he provided.

Milton Wong's ability to bridge within and between communities, cultures, faiths and generations, as well as across boundaries, was an invisible art that wove you in. Before you knew it, you were caught in his enthusiastic embrace, and your journey in a common cause had begun. Milt was a true listener, humble and empathetic, building trust and uniting people around shared goals. At the same time, he encouraged and created space for personal growth and achievement; he was challenging but always supportive, channelling new ideas and energy beyond personal ambition for positive societal change. Distance was no bar. Even though in the last several years my career took me to the mountain regions of Central Asia, we remained connected throughout. Our exchanges took on a more global dimension and the urgent need for better understanding in our increasingly interdependent but fragile world. I will remember Milton for his eternal optimism and his faith that the intrinsic goodness in people was simply waiting to be ignited.

Nurjehan Mawani *is currently the diplomatic representative of the Aga Khan Development Network (AKDN) in the Kyrgyz Republic. She joined the AKDN after a long and distinguished career in the Canadian public service and has received numerous awards in recognition of her contribution to public service and her profession, including the Order of Canada and the Outstanding Achievement Award of the Public Service of Canada. She is a lawyer and was in private practice with Clark Wilson LLP in Vancouver prior to joining the public service.*

An original Singer sewing machine from Modernize Tailors, opened in 1913 by Milton's father Wong Kung Lai. In its heyday, Modernize Tailors was the hub of Vancouver's Chinatown and customers came from all over the city to be fitted for the latest fashions, like zoot suits. Milton grew up helping his father in the shop, first by sweeping floors and later helping measure and fit customers for pants. Over the years, Modernize Tailors made suits for men from all walks of life—from lawyers on lunch break to loggers on vacation from months in the bush. Later with the growth of the Vancouver film industry, Modernize made suits for Sean Connery and Arnold Schwarzenegger, among others. In 2006, when the building that originally housed Modernize came up for sale, Milton purchased and restored it to ensure that the tailor shop would continue to have a home in its historic location in Chinatown.

Singer Sewing Machine
1916

JOHN ROBINSON

How to Change the World

DON'T REMEMBER HOW the conversation started, but I do remember Milt saying to me: "We have to get you and Bruce Sampson and a few others up to our place on Quadra to talk about how to move this idea forward. And you must bring your partners: sustainability is about social relationships also." I am not sure I have the words exactly right, but I know that they accurately convey two things about Milton Wong that were central to any interaction I ever had with him. In the first place, Milt was always about moving things forward, finding a way to make progress and creating positive action. Secondly, Milt always emphasized, indeed insisted on, the crucial importance of the human dimensions of sustainability. If there was any statement that I heard him make many times, it was "Values! We have to make values the central component of sustainability."

In this case, the idea Milt was referring to was one that a few of us had been working on for several years. We wanted to create a building at the University of British Columbia that would be a living laboratory, a place where we could implement, practise, study and teach sustainability at the building and the regional scale. At this time, 2004, CIRS—the Centre for Interactive Research on Sustainability—seemed to face some pretty significant obstacles. Milt's solution was to invite me; my wife, Deborah; Bruce and Emmy Sampson; and several other colleagues to his resort on Quadra Island to brainstorm about how best to move our CIRS agenda— and the related agendas of our colleagues—forward. He flew us all up to Quadra and put us up there for the weekend. We spent three days with

Milt and Fei, eating the great food they prepared and thinking through the challenges we faced.

It is hard to describe just how important that gesture of Milt's was. At a low point in the CIRS story, it re-energized us. It gave us a sense of possibility and renewed purpose. It provided fresh ideas for a process that had gone slightly stale. Perhaps most importantly, the faith that Milt and Fei showed in our ideas, their generous and open hospitality and the conviction they displayed that this problem could be worked out by getting a few good people together made a lasting positive impression and taught me an important lesson about promoting social change. We returned refreshed to the battle, and today, I am very happy to report my office is in the new CIRS building, which had its official opening on November 3, 2011.

The views I have attributed to Milt were characteristic of all of our discussions. He never wavered in his belief that we needed to think about the big picture, that we could create a better world and that this would be done by working together in a supportive way, in the service of those values we shared. He put ideas into action in a tireless series of social interventions and service to his community. One afternoon a month before CIRS opened, I got a call from Milt. "John," he said, "I am calling to put you in touch with my friend here, who manufactures energy-efficient lighting in China." He then put his friend on the line, in the sure knowledge that connecting people is an essential part of creating a more sustainable world.

I owe a lot to Milt, as so many do. Perhaps the most important things he taught me were to think big and never give up on a sustainable future.

John Robinson is associate provost, sustainability, and a professor in the Institute for Resources, Environment and Sustainability and the Department of Geography at the University of British Columbia.

One of the
Good Guys

MILTON WONG WAS truly one of the good guys. A businessman who generously believed in using his wealth and success to build better communities and a better world, Milton was loved and respected in Vancouver and beyond.

Death waits for all of us, but it came far too soon for Milton Wong. His life was a classic story of new Canadian families, moving from poverty to financial success through intelligence and hard work. Having achieved wealth, Milton proceeded to share it to further the causes he believed in. I was always impressed by his understanding that community and personal well-being are critical for a truly rich and sustainable society. His ethnic background and experience were an intimate part of his activities and the causes he supported. When he spoke about the importance of the environment, he never saw it as something separate from issues of social justice and democracy. It's no surprise that he was deeply concerned with First Nations in Canada. He worked on many projects to establish connections between businesses and First Nations and helped with First Nations land claims agreements, including the historic Nisga'a Treaty in 1998. He was also a good friend to the David Suzuki Foundation, offering us support and even criticism when it was warranted.

Milton loved the ocean, and he supported our work to restore the productivity and abundance that existed in Georgia Strait only a few decades ago. Everything he did, whether supporting dragon boat racing, serving as chancellor of SFU or creating an ecologically designed garden and house on

A BUSINESSMAN *who generously*

believed in using his wealth

and success to build better

communities and a better world.

Quadra Island, he did with panache and passion. It was a privilege to know Milton. He, his wife, Fei, and their three daughters have been role models for all of us. His passing was a tragic loss for Canada.

David Suzuki is an award-winning scientist, environmentalist and broadcaster. A world leader in sustainable ecology, he was named one of UNEP's Global 500 and is the recipient of UNESCO's Kalinga Prize for the Popularization of Science and the United Nations Environment Programme medal. In 2009, he won the Right Livelihood Award, known widely as the "Alternative Nobel Prize."

This photograph by nephew Dave Robertson was
purchased by Fei and Milton at Dave's first show at Becker
Galleries in Vancouver. Fei and Milton often chose art
together, not just as a gesture to support young artists
but as a more meaningful alternative to buying each other
jewellery or more frivolous gifts. After their engagement,
Milton famously exclaimed to Fei that her engagement
ring was the "first and last" piece of jewellery he would
buy her.

Block Watch Area, Mathias Rd.
DAVE ROBERTSON | 2009

Educating the Heart

MILTON WONG CAME to mind immediately when I first encountered the magnificent Four Great Rivers project in Tibet in 2005. I was there to see if the David Suzuki Foundation could play a role in helping to preserve one of the world's most important and pristine ecosystems.

At 46 million acres—the size of Italy—covering two prefectures in the Himalayas, the project encompasses the fourth-largest protected area in the world. It holds the source of four of the world's greatest rivers: the Brahmaputra, the Salween, the Mekong and the Yangtze. The eight countries downstream are home to 20 per cent of all humanity—more than 1 billion people.

The region's steep river valleys, covered in lush forest, are more stunning than anything I have ever seen. The Brahmaputra gorge is four times deeper than the Grand Canyon, and the area's biodiversity is almost unmatched in Asia. The area is also home to 800,000 Tibetans, most of them living in poverty and subsisting on very little. I knew that any effort to protect the ecosystem there would need to closely involve the people.

"Milton will get this," I said to myself, and sure enough, he did.

Back in Vancouver a couple of weeks later, I started talking to people about the project. The DSF needed guidance and financial help to support its involvement in Tibet. Of the many business and community leaders I called, Milton was the only one who understood right away what I was talking about: building sustainable communities in a remote part of the world as part of the project to protect an important natural ecosystem. Within days, he had not only made a personal financial contribution but convinced Simon Fraser University to do so as well. With some additional funding from the DSF, we now had the seed money to get started.

Without Milton's active and enthusiastic support at the outset, the project as we envisaged it would not have been possible. When I returned to Tibet three years later with the DSF's president, Tara Cullis, to review what progress had been made, it was clear that a solid foundation had been laid and that our vision—and Milton's—was being realized.

Of course, it didn't surprise me that Milton was so supportive of the project. We'd been good friends for many years, and I knew how passionate he was about protecting and preserving our fragile planet. I also knew the depth of his compassion for humanity and his willingness to be involved in helping communities lift themselves up.

His commitment to our project was illustrated quite humorously some time later at a function in Vancouver. Milton was being honoured by the Aga Khan Foundation, and he was in the middle of his acceptance speech. When he looked up and noticed me in the audience, he stopped in mid-sentence, as if he had lost his train of thought. When he started speaking again, he talked about the Four Great Rivers project in Tibet and enthused about its success.

Years before I met Milton, I read a news report in which he mentioned that his hero was David Suzuki. That wasn't just talk. Milton's actions over the years clearly demonstrated a passion for social justice and a love for humanity and the natural world that paralleled David's views.

It often struck me that Milton had a very unusual—perhaps unique—combination of qualities: he was a visionary with a big heart and a sharp mind; he had the ability to process information and understand complexities quickly; he was compassionate and caring; and he was generous, not only with financial support but also with his time and guidance.

I always regarded Milton as a mentor. He taught me so much of what I know about educating the heart, a concept the Dalai Lama espouses, and he inspired me to strive for distant goals I might otherwise have abandoned. I have never known anyone with a bigger heart than Milton's, and the goals he reached in his own life set benchmarks that very few of us will ever achieve.

Jim Hoggan *is one of Canada's most respected public relations professionals and the president and owner of Hoggan & Associates, an award-winning strategic communications firm specializing in crisis management and stakeholder engagement for government, industry and not-for-profit organizations. He serves as a trustee of the Dalai Lama Center for Peace and Education; is the chair of the David Suzuki Foundation; and is a co-founder of both the Stonehouse Standing Circle, an innovative public engagement and communications think tank, and the influential site DeSmogBlog, which works to clean up industry and government misinformation about environmental issues.*

Brought to Quadra
by Bluebacks

Milton Wong once told me how
his eyes lit up seeing a school of bluebacks swim beneath the dock
of a resort he was staying at while visiting Quadra Island years ago.
That would spark up the chance to make it his own
build in its background the most fantastic home
working around the trees
in elegant magnificence,
looking like a natural hillside from the air,
grandeur, without imposing,
the design of a strong and gentle spirit.
It was a fortunate day many years ago
somewhere north of Nanaimo
as dark shadows and rain began to fall
he picked me up hitchhiking going to Heriot Bay
saying, "I own a resort right by there."
Where years later, I would tie up at the dock
followed by crows and seagulls in a squawking admiring flock
to regularly supply prawns for his family dinners
along with the garden at the top of the hill, grown organically
    especially for them
right beside the campground
where they allowed Cash Bailey a peaceful, pleasant home
in the years of his decline.

Milton was a man who saw the precious value of this community
who did a lot to keep Quadra the way that it is
with character and style, the way that we all love it
while progress wreaks havoc elsewhere,
possibly discussed and done in the social circles he would likely encounter.
Here was the man who said he was never going to retire
dreaming up new ideas and ways to stay in the game
using his personal power to contribute to the greater good
in more ways than he probably was ever aware of
donating land for the community garden
Quadra's own field of dreams
where those who never owned land feel their roots sprout in the dirt
consisting of a purple-and-white bulb.
I honour Milton Wong growing a curly green flower
which is eaten more than admired,
picked before it blooms
giving health, spice and flavour
adding fire to the meal.
I'm talking garlic here, some kind of special strain
that grew in rows in the old horse pasture
whispering of true freedom, including the source of one's food
reaching out to others through preparing it with pride and celebration.
Saying of all the boats he'd ever owned
it was the simple outboard-powered tin skiff that gave him the
     most enjoyment.
It was the one he wanted to keep forever.

As he walked through this world as a person of importance
with unassuming elegance and delight in the magic of life
expanding upon the dream by giving others a chance

we honour him now
and give thanks
for having had Milton Wong among us,
a man who set foot upon the shores of Quadra
with the care with which he touched the island and all of our lives,
brought here by a school of blueback coho years ago.
We say goodbye to a true friend, whom I myself barely knew.

Rena Patrick *is a Quadra Island poet who works as a deckhand on a local prawn boat, has a plot at the community garden and stays at Taku during the prawn season. She has a radio show on Cortes radio, lives on her own sailboat, works part-time on lighthouses in the winter and appreciates the unique lifestyle of the island.*

Milton played a major role in moving
forward many First Nations initiatives
and helped to structure land claim and
business partnerships for groups across
B.C. He played a pivotal role in galvanizing
support within B.C.'s business community for
the signing of the historic Nisga'a Treaty.

Big Ideas
with Heart

FOLLOWING MILTON WONG'S passing, English and Chinese media outlets across Canada highlighted the loss of a great business leader and philanthropist. They applauded Milton's enormous impact on the world: his championing of multiculturalism, social justice, sustainability and the arts and his compassion for the people living in Vancouver's Downtown Eastside. They reviewed Milton's success as an entrepreneur and an angel investor. No one, however, identified Milton's immeasurable impact on the world of ideas, his influence on the country's biggest thinkers. He pushed for the support of Aboriginal causes long before the federal government apologized for the Indian residential schools. He advocated for "cultural accommodation" at a time when pervasive anti-immigrant sentiment was directed at the wave of immigrants from Hong Kong. He informed leaders in the financial sector that there is no such thing as unlimited growth. These were provocative ideas. Today, the concept of multiculturalism seems outdated, sustainability is politically hip and the Occupy movement showed us that Milton was right about the myth of unlimited growth.

For me, Milton Wong was nothing short of a superhero. I was proud to know him as a mentor and a friend, but I mostly knew him as a larger-than-life person with the charisma and fearlessness of one who could to leap from building to building.

Like all superheroes, Milton was always on the move. If not physically, then mentally. His brain never seemed to rest. He also had an acute passion for young people with big ideas. He loved helping them make things happen.

HE HAD a way of making you feel you were the newest and brightest star in the sky and then pushing you to shine.

Milton mentored people in their twenties, their thirties, their forties and their fifties. He saw them all as "young people." He had a way of making you feel you were the newest and brightest star in the sky and then pushing you to shine.

In 2007, Milton was invited to speak at an important policy conference about multiculturalism. Maybe because he was so focussed on Vancouver's Downtown Eastside at the time, he felt a little out of touch with the issue. So he invited me to lunch. Rather than drawing on my ideas, he said he was going to insist that the conference organizers let me speak alongside him.

At the reception the evening before the conference, Milton came up to me and asked, "So, are you ready?" "I think so," I said, expecting him to follow up with some words of encouragement. I was trying to stay calm. This annual conference was a high-profile event. I'd just learned that the idea for NATO had been hatched at a similar gathering years earlier. Instead, Milton looked me straight in the eye and said, "Alden, we get one shot tomorrow. Just one shot. That's it."

I put down my unfinished glass of wine, went back to my room and rehearsed until 2:30 in the morning. Milton had put me on the spot, but he was right. That one speech of ours has since turned into seventy-five related presentations across Canada and in four other countries.

Milton's momentum made him unpredictable. I always had a game plan, because you never knew what direction a meeting with him would take. It was like an ant trying to steer a lion. You might meet wanting career advice and leave with a book to read, marriage advice or even a new suit. His marriage advice? He had only one tip: "Remember, compromise means different things to different people." Absolute wisdom.

One of Milton's many secrets was that he surrounded himself with people he saw, and openly credited, as being smarter than he was. He also had an uncanny ability to mobilize the biggest brains and the busiest people to make "something out of nothing." He loved that phrase. Milton repeatedly pointed out that we are all connected. We are connected to each other, to the past and to the future. And in that lay his superpower: he linked people—to ideas, certainly, but most importantly to other people. He was a very busy superhero.

MILTON WAS OFTEN referred to as a social entrepreneur, but I thought of him more as a compassionate entrepreneur. As he turned his attention to Vancouver's Downtown Eastside, he petitioned the business community to act with heart, to build their towers with heart, to make money with heart. The last big speech he and I were slated to write together was on something he called the "era of stewardship." It brought together his ideas on multiculturalism and social justice and his passion for sustainability. He explained to me that, as we endeavour to be stewards of our oceans and forests, stewardship has to include people—we are the stewards of each other.

One day, Milton shared the germ of an idea that I could tell perplexed him. I knew he wasn't clear in his mind about how to make this idea happen. He was envisioning a place in Vancouver's Downtown Eastside where homeless people could come to wash and receive medical care for their feet. He asked me, "Do you know why we see so many homeless people off their feet? It's because their feet are in really bad shape." As he spoke, I imagined this great man washing the feet of Vancouver's most in need. It was a profound and humbling vision. Not necessarily to end homelessness but to enact stewardship. His big ideas weren't just big but meaningful and practical on a human level.

It was years before I thought about his foot care idea again, and it came to me quite unexpectedly. When I saw Milton for the last time, he asked me to help him tie his shoelaces as he got ready to leave the hospital for home. His feet were slightly swollen. He said nothing as I loosely tied his laces, but I remembered his idea. I felt him asking how willing I would be to do the same for others in the years to come.

Your prosperity is my prosperity, Milton wanted us to remember. Your struggle is my struggle, whether we know each other or not. This simple but profound idea, planted deep in the hearts of the many people whose lives he touched, is his legacy—an achievement worthy of a true superhero.

Alden E. Habacon *is a diversity and inclusion specialist, an international speaker and a consultant. In 2010, he was appointed director of intercultural understanding strategy development for the University of British Columbia. He is founding publisher of* Schema Magazine *(SchemaMag.ca) and co-founder of the Asian Canadian Journalists Association (ACJA) of Vancouver.*

MILTON K. WONG
Canadian-Style Multiculturalism

PRESENTED TO THE COUCHICHING INSTITUTE ON
PUBLIC AFFAIRS ANNUAL SUMMER CONFERENCE: "THE STRANGER
NEXT DOOR: MAKING DIVERSITY WORK," AUGUST 9, 2007

IT'S A TALL order, being asked to speak at length about cultural diversity, the survival of the planet and how pluralism and sustainability may be the emerging common moral sentiments that will lay the foundation for a positive future for mankind. There's something a little bit *War and Peace* about such a weighty, daunting topic.

But seriously, I've been thinking and speaking about multiculturalism for many years, and never has it been more important to understand the contribution it can make to a peaceful world. So I'm going to offer some opening remarks that will, I hope, give you the background and perspective you'll need to fully appreciate what my friend Alden Habacon is going to talk about after me.

When I first began to be intellectually preoccupied with multiculturalism, I was quite fascinated with the metaphor of the tapestry used to describe the Canadian model. And all these years later, I still think that metaphor works beautifully. We still receive a quarter of a million new immigrants every year—that's the highest immigration rate in the world, by the way—and we continue to add them to the tapestry.

Their unique identities are what make the tapestry attractive in its entirety, yet we never fully lose sight of the individual strands. That's the beauty of it. We are, I believe, a resilient and vibrant nation because of our immigrants.

Canadian multiculturalism has also been called a mosaic. Either way, it's about celebrating and protecting diversity in our society in a way that produces a harmonious and united result.

You might wonder how multiculturalism is different from pluralism, another often-discussed term. A standard definition of pluralism is this: a state or society in which members of diverse ethnic, racial, religious or social groups maintain an autonomous participation in, and development of, their traditional culture or special interest within the confines of a common civilization.

We could quibble over the subtle differences between multiculturalism and pluralism. Personally, I believe pluralism is more specific and less nebulous than what is implied by multiculturalism. Pluralism takes a stronger position. It clearly assigns diverse cultural groups autonomous identities to which they can adhere while at the same time living in agreement with some of the ground rules that describe Canadian citizenship. For some time now, I've believed pluralism is the direction we've been taking in Canadian society—and I believe it's the right direction for Canada.

Of course, not everyone agrees with me. Some people lean towards a more American-style melting pot concept. Some would prefer a model in between—more cultural intermingling than what pluralism describes but not quite the "melting point." And then there's what I'll call the postmodern view of ethnic diversity, which Alden is going to talk about.

But personally, I have always found wisdom in the writings of Charles Taylor, a Canadian philosopher and writer who has studied the formation of human identity and who believes in the necessity of multiculturalism. Taylor distinguishes between two traditions in liberal democratic theory: on the one hand, the politics of equal dignity, based on the notion that all humans deserve respect and equal rights universally and equally; and on the other hand, the politics of difference, based on the notion that all humans— including individuals and groups—need and deserve recognition of their unique identities.

These two perspectives might appear to contradict each other at first. The former requires treating people in a difference-blind manner, whereas the latter demands differential treatment. Yet Taylor maintains that these perspectives are compatible because they are both built on the notion of equal respect.

Taylor has written that humans create their identities dialogically: that is, in relation to others. According to this theory, since human identity is at least partly shaped by recognition, when recognition is withheld, it can damage a person's dignity. The same can be said for groups of people who share a common identity. To extrapolate, for instance, if we fail to recognize the Aboriginals' claim to a unique identity, we injure their dignity.

Due recognition, according to Taylor, is not simply a courtesy, but a vital human need. Taylor's multiculturalism is a logical extension of the politics of equal respect and recognition. In his words, "All human cultures that have animated whole societies over some considerable stretch of time have something important to say to all human beings."

My impression that immigrants make us stronger as a nation also seems to be supported by research done recently by Environics president Michael Adams. In his latest book, *Unlikely Utopia,* Adams shows that the percentage of ethnic minorities participating in the political process is higher here in Canada than in other countries. To me, that's proof that our process of accommodation works. And it's evidence of how we differentiate ourselves from other countries that are perhaps less welcoming of immigrants or less accommodating of differences.

Because of this success, a question has long preoccupied academics, journalists and political leaders interested in the Canadian approach to multiculturalism: How did we get to where we are today? And how can other countries learn from our example?

Some people seem to have the impression that Canadian multiculturalism was a deliberate experiment based on intellectual discussions and decisions about how to shape our society. But I would argue that it has been more of a happy accident—a serendipitous outcome based on historical events.

Before I elaborate, I will tell you that not all of these ideas are mine; many come from John Ralston Saul's book *Reflections of a Siamese Twin:*

Canada at the Beginning of the Twenty-first Century. So I want to give him credit for that. When I opened that book and started reading more about some of the early events in Canadian history, I realized that they give us a sneak preview, so to speak—or call it a foreshadowing—of modern multiculturalism. It seems to me that the Canada we know today owes much of the nature of its existence to the partnership of two men: Robert Baldwin and Louis LaFontaine.

Both men were lawyers. LaFontaine's political career began at the age of twenty-three, when he was elected to the Legislative Assembly of Lower Canada. He was known for his dedication to French Canada. Baldwin also entered politics early in life, motivated by a desire to change the Canadian political system.

Early in nineteenth-century Canada, elites dominated the British colonies of Upper and Lower Canada. They were smugly content with their positions of privilege, supported by British governors and paid scant attention to the elected assemblies of the colonies. I will simplify things a bit here, but essentially, the complacency of these elites, their lack of willingness to engage with the elected assemblies, eventually generated a great deal of resentment among the colonies. When that resentment peaked, rebellions broke out in Upper and Lower Canada. Rebellion was quickly defeated in Upper Canada, but it was long and bloody in Lower Canada.

When the fighting ended, the British government sent a representative to investigate the colonial grievances. The report that went back to the government prescribed greater power and autonomy for the colonial assemblies, exactly what the Lower Canadian rebels had been fighting for. But it also recommended that Upper and Lower Canada be united, a proposal that many Lower Canadians adamantly opposed. If this story is starting to sound familiar, you probably know that Lower Canada is now known as Quebec.

Nevertheless, in winter of 1841, a union between the two areas was proclaimed and elections were called. LaFontaine ran in a Quebec riding called Terrebonne. But on election day, two hundred armed thugs prevented his supporters from voting, and he lost the election.

Meanwhile, Baldwin had been elected in two different ridings in what is now the Toronto area. He met with constituents in one of those ridings—Fourth York—to see if they would agree to elect LaFontaine in his place. Then he sent LaFontaine a letter asking if he would agree to run in a by-election in Toronto. LaFontaine agreed. He campaigned in Toronto on a platform of French-English cooperation and easily won his seat. Meanwhile, Baldwin's gesture of goodwill garnered him francophone support in Lower Canada.

And that is how, in the absence of any specific design to unite the French and the English in Canada, Baldwin and LaFontaine unwittingly sowed the first seeds of a nation that would eventually celebrate the relatively peaceful co-existence of two cultures and two languages. A respected francophone journalist of the time, Étienne Parent, wrote: "If all the inhabitants of Upper Canada are like [Baldwin], I predict the most brilliant results of the Union of the Canadas."

My point is that whether they knew it or not, Baldwin and LaFontaine planted a seed when they shook hands. That seed grew into an unusual, uniquely Canadian form of multiculturalism. It grew into a Canada founded on the union of two distinctly different cultures to combat a mutual adversary. The ability to embrace that which is different—to work together towards common goals, despite cultural and linguistic differences—is at the heart of Canadian multiculturalism.

By Confederation in 1867, accommodating the French language, culture, laws and religion was a matter of fact, not a matter for debate. Canada had been built on a revolutionary commitment to cooperation and compromise. The requirement for accommodation was an inherent feature of the Baldwin-LaFontaine agreement. That requirement was built into our constitution officially in 1982, but what's more important is that it is also built intuitively into our behaviour. Multiculturalism in Canada has truly been an organic, grassroots process.

It might not be a stretch to suggest that as Canadians, cultural tolerance is one of the defining features of our national "collective unconscious." In other words, it isn't something we make a conscious effort to practise or think about every time we get up in the morning. Instead, it's just there, invisible in the background, framing the way we think about our lives, our country and our common value system.

There never was a grand, deliberate experiment. No, Canadian multiculturalism really defies reductionism. Its beauty is in its complexity. However, that doesn't mean we shouldn't take some pride in how we've managed the unique brand of multiculturalism that evolved from historical events. History may have created it, but as a society we have made choices about how to support and encourage it.

And perhaps no one is more interested in how we've pulled this off than the Aga Khan. As a member of the board of directors of the Aga Khan Foundation Canada, I've had lots of opportunities to familiarize myself with the Aga Khan's work in international development around the world. The Aga Khan has looked at multiculturalism in Canada and concluded that the Canadian way of life is a model that should be studied and copied in other parts of the world to promote peace.

He believes, and so do I, that countries around the world have much to understand about how we've fused a diverse nation together so peacefully here in Canada.

That's why he is establishing the Global Centre for Pluralism in Ottawa. The centre is founded on the idea that "tolerance, openness and understanding towards the cultures, social structures, values and faiths of other peoples are now essential to the very survival of an interdependent world." One of the central reasons for the centre's existence is the Aga Khan's belief that "pluralism is no longer simply an asset or a prerequisite for progress and development. It is vital to our existence."

The Aga Khan's interest in Canadian multiculturalism was sparked back in the 1970s, when many Ismailis, seeking refuge from ethnic strife in East

Africa, were welcomed by Canadian communities. As the Ismailis' spiritual leader, the Aga Khan was interested in understanding how Canada had succeeded so well at managing diversity. He began asking Canadian leaders about it. Then, several years ago, he launched a formal pluralism initiative to better understand how Canadian multiculturalism works and how its lessons could be shared with other culturally diverse societies.

The Global Centre for Pluralism is meant to function as an international centre of excellence for the study, practice and teaching of pluralism. Because of his belief that Canada "epitomizes what can be achieved through a commitment to pluralism," the Aga Khan has committed $30 million of his own money towards this project, describing the Canadian commitment to finding unity in diversity as "Canada's gift to the world."

Of course, pluralism needs the right context to establish itself successfully, to grow strong roots and blossom. It has to be based on dignity and equal opportunity—on population-based health care and education systems, for example. Values and systems like these are what allow pluralism to develop and thrive. Without them, pluralism cannot exist.

I believe the Aga Khan Foundation of Canada and the Global Centre for Pluralism offer Canadians concrete ways to participate in sharing what we have and what we have learned. They are a way for the future. In fact, I think that because of the increasingly global nature of our world, pluralism and sustainability may join hands to become the twin central emerging common values that are capable of bringing peaceful unity to diverse communities.

Because of the precarious state of our planet, it is quickly becoming apparent to people everywhere that a massive cooperative effort will be needed if we want to rescue our Earth from a devastating tipping point. We will need to put our differences aside and work towards a common purpose. That's why I feel that the challenge of saving the world from climate collapse and other environmental disasters has the potential to soften the cultural differences that once divided us. Slowly but surely, it is becoming apparent that no matter where we come from, what we look like, what religion we practise or what language we speak, we are in this together. If I buy a Chevrolet Suburban and drive it across Canada several times, the impact will be felt one way or another on the other side of the world.

This is a brand-new phenomenon in modern history. The world has never felt quite so small. Looking at the world through the lens of sustainability, you see that everyone has the same DNA; you realize suddenly that at the cellular level, we're all the same. When you think about it this way, it seems unfathomable that, around the world, so many people seem to have so much trouble respecting each other and respecting the planet.

Years ago, when I was working on land claims issues with the Nisga'a, I was at Joseph Gosnell's home for breakfast one morning. As chief negotiator for the Nisga'a people, Joseph was responsible for the signing of the historic Nisga'a Treaty in 1999. That morning, I said to him, "Joe, according to some research I've seen, the Aboriginals may have come from central China, over the land bridge to Alaska and down to South America." I remarked that maybe I had a stronger right to land claims than he did. I was only joking, of course, but I thought this theory added a whole new dimension, not only to the land claims and Aboriginal rights issues we were discussing but to my understanding of how, as human beings on this planet, we really are all related.

So yes, we all share the same DNA—science tells us that. At the same time, multiculturalism is based on recognizing and respecting social behaviours, customs and values that are different from each other. Yet I don't see a contradiction here. Socially and emotionally, there are more important ways in which we're all the same than there are ways in which we differ. For example, all human beings love their children and want the best for them. What they mean by "best" may differ according to culture. But the fundamental impulse is the same everywhere you go.

And, increasingly, more of us around the world are recognizing the importance of sustainable living. It is an emerging common social value, one that I believe has the potential to unite us despite cultural differences. The need for us to work as a united global society towards a common goal, whose achievement will mean nothing less than the survival of our planet, may have a powerful harmonizing effect on the way we relate to each other.

Alden Habacon, who is about to replace me here at the podium, has some very interesting thoughts on taking multiculturalism to new and exciting places. He's going to explain how Canada is already going beyond pluralism to a whole new view of diversity, to where ethnicity begins to encompass other facets of identity, such as people's values—like sustainable living. The idea of pluralism and sustainability working shoulder to shoulder to unite us in our diversity and promote cultural harmony around the world is an exciting one indeed. Perhaps decades from now, if we succeed in that lofty goal, we'll have pluralism to thank for setting us on the right path, and sustainability for keeping us there.

Call it Canadian-style multiculturalism, call it pluralism, call it Alden Habacon's vision of ethnic identity: it's essential for world peace. Or, as His Highness the Aga Khan has said, "We cannot make the world safe for democracy unless we also make the world safe for diversity." These are big, bold statements, but I believe they are absolutely true.

ACKNOWLEDGEMENTS

OUR HEARTFELT thank you to the following individuals. Without your contributions and support, this book would not exist: the numerous contributors, who so generously gave their time and shared their special moments with the rest of us, including those whose stories and interviews were not included in this book; the team at Greystone Books, who guided this process with grace and wisdom, notably Rob Sanders, Carra Simpson and Shirarose Wilensky for being true partners of this project; a special thank you to Barbara Pulling for making sense of an unformed idea and giving this book its shape; the designers Peter Cocking and Jessica Sullivan for their vision and creativity; Maurice Wong for his unwavering support in the materializing of this idea; Dave Robertson for his beautiful photography of Milton and Fei's private art collection; the transcribers Christina Jung, Joy Kim and Zi-Ann Lum, whose efforts gave us the essential material; John Montalbano for his invaluable mentorship and strategic advice; Ann Cowan for pointing us in the right direction at the earliest stages of this project; Rio Tinto Alcan Dragon Boat Festival for staging the announcement of the book; Fei Wong for sharing, with great attention to detail, Milton's life and passion; the entire Wong family for their loving and unsparing support; and Milton K. Wong for having a vision for this book and entrusting Elizabeth Wong, Joanna Wong and Alden E. Habacon to see it through.

CREDITS